Living in Christ

The Paschal Mystery

Christ's Mission of Salvation

Brian Singer-Towns

saint mary's press

The Subcommittee on the Catechism, United States Conference of Catholic Bishops, has found that this catechetical high school text, copyright 2011, is in conformity with the *Catechism of the Catholic Church* and that it fulfills the requirements of Course III: "The Mission of Jesus Christ (The Paschal Mystery)" of the *Doctrinal Elements of a Curriculum Framework for the Development of Catechetical Materials for Young People of High School Age.*

Nihil Obstat: Rev. William M. Becker, STD
                  Censor Librorum
                  November 12, 2010
Imprimatur: † Most Rev. John M. Quinn, DD
                  Bishop of Winona
                  November 12, 2010

The nihil obstat and imprimatur are official declarations that a book or pamphlet is free of doctrinal or moral error. No implication is contained therein that those who have granted the nihil obstat or imprimatur agree with the contents, opinions, or statements expressed, nor do they assume any legal responsibility associated with publication.

The publishing team included Brian Singer-Towns, development editor; Steven McGlaun, contributing editor; Maura Thompson Hagarty, contributing editor and theological reviewer; Chris Wardwell, contributing author; prepress and manufacturing coordinated by the production departments of Saint Mary's Press.

Cover Image: © The Crosiers/Gene Plaisted, OSC

Printed in the United States of America

1147 (PO4169)

ISBN 978-1-59982-058-3, Print

Contents

Section 2: Jesus Christ's Mission Is Revealed

Section 3: God's Plan for Salvation Is Fulfilled

Section 4: The Paschal Mystery and Your Life

Section 5: Prayer and the Paschal Mystery

Introduction

As a young man I spent several years searching for something I didn't know I had lost. From birth I grew up in a devout Catholic family, as a teen I served as an altar server and lector in my parish, and as a college student I continued to attend Mass every Sunday. But after a while, I felt like I was just going through the motions. If you were to see the brave face I presented to the world, you would have thought I was just fine. But inside I was a confused and lonely person.

What I didn't know then was that deep inside myself, in my soul, I was missing a crucial connection with God. I tried to fill that void in many ways. I tried making new friends, joining new groups, and reading about different religions. But it wasn't until I joined a Bible study group that was reading the Gospel of Mark that I found what my soul was missing: a close and intimate relationship with the Trinity—the Father, Son, and Holy Spirit.

I share this story because there is a danger in writing a textbook about Jesus Christ. The danger is that it can make faith in Jesus seem like just another intellectual exercise, just another subject to master on your way to adulthood. Yet as I discovered those many years ago, yes, faith involves the intellect, but there is more to it. God wants to be in an intimate relationship of love with each of us. He has worked throughout history to reveal that desire and make it possible for us to bridge the "gap" that separates us from his love.

The Paschal Mystery is the name we give to the process of God's plan of salvation, which is principally accomplished through the life, death, Resurrection, and Ascension of Jesus Christ. This book explores that plan, from its beginnings in the Garden of Eden to its glorious conclusion at the Parousia. We will see how God has been at work throughout all of history to restore what was lost—our full and intimate communion with the Holy Trinity. Perhaps most important, we will look at how God calls each of us to be active participants in his plan.

When I gave myself over in faith to God's loving invitation those many years ago, my whole life was renewed. I discovered a deeper and more profound relationship with God. And because of that, I entered into deeper and more loving relationships with other people. My faith in Christ saves me from sin and will save me from death. It saves me from confusion, loneliness, and despair. Every day it gives my life meaning, joy, and hope even when times are hard and when bad things happen. As a member of the Body of Christ, the Church, I have met and been loved by many amazing and wonderful people, people who inspire me to deeper commitment in my journey of faith.

That is what I wish for you. I hope that as you study this student book, you take what it teaches about Jesus Christ and the Paschal Mystery seriously. There is an important intellectual dimension to belief. We must believe in the right things, the truths revealed by God. But I also hope this will be more than an intellectual exercise for you. I pray that you will let the love of Christ that is expressed in the Paschal Mystery touch your heart and motivate your every action. I pray that you will see your study of the Paschal Mystery as an invitation from God to draw closer to him and to let this Mystery become the spiritual center of your life. Let God fill the hunger in your soul.

Blessings,
Brian Singer-Towns

God's Plan for Salvation: The Big Picture

Part 1

The Goodness of Creation

God has a plan and *you* are a part of it. Modern science has come a long way in explaining the creation, the growth, and even the end of stars and galaxies. We have some very intriguing theories, such as the big bang theory, about how the universe came into existence. Through the gift of our intellect, we can continue to learn about the workings of the universe; through faith we know that it was created by God.

God created the universe out of love. His creation is good, and God loves all of it, every photon, every grain of sand, every blade of grass, and every form of life that swims, crawls, walks, or flies. And in his plan human beings have a special place. God has made us "little less than a god, \ crowned . . . with glory and honor" (Psalm 8:6). God has a plan and *you* are a part of it.

The topics covered in this part are:

- Article 1: "The Primeval History" (page 11)

- Article 2: "Creation Reflects the Glory of God" (page 14)

- Article 3: "Human Beings: The Summit of Creation" (page 17)

- Article 4: "The Garden of Eden: The Perfect Life" (page 21)

Article 1 The Primeval History

As we explore God's plan, it makes sense to start with his intention in creating the world in the first place. Was God bored? Was God lonely? Was he looking for some free labor? No, no, and no! The creation stories of other ancient cultures claimed these as reasons for why the gods created the earth and human beings. But the two creation accounts in Sacred Scripture, found in the first two chapters of the Book of Genesis, give very different reasons. This is why the first two chapters of Genesis have a special place in teaching us about creation. These chapters contain the familiar accounts of the six days of creation, the creation of Adam and Eve, and Adam and Eve's fall from grace.

Although the two accounts of creation originated at different times, both reveal important truths about God. In the accounts of creation, God is revealed as the one, true God, who sustains the whole universe. He created the world out of love, because he is Love. He created the world to be good, because he is Goodness. He revealed the serpent's words as lies, because he is Truth. Even after Adam and Eve's sin, God's love for humanity remains steadfast and faithful, because he is Faithfulness.

The two creation accounts are part of a section of Genesis, chapters 1–11, called "The Primeval History" in some Bibles. *Primeval* sounds like *prehistoric,* and it means kind of the same thing. **Primeval history** means that these are symbolic accounts about things that happened long before we have any historical records—written or **archaeological**—of any kind. These texts probably came from several different ancient Jewish sources. Under the inspiration of the Holy Spirit, these stories were told, refined, and edited together over the course of several centuries before they became the final text we have today. In the primeval history, God is revealing some very important truths. We will take a closer look at those truths in the next articles.

primeval history
The time before the invention of writing and recording of historical data.

archaeology
The scientific study of the material remains of past human life.

© Robert Simon/iStockphoto.com

figurative language

A literary form that uses symbolic images, stories, and names to point to a deeper truth.

literary forms (genres)

Different kinds of writing determined by their literary technique, content, tone, and purpose (how the author wants the reader to be affected).

Religious Truth and Scientific Truth

The primeval history in the Sacred Scripture teaches religious truth, not science. We know this because these chapters are written in figurative language (see the "Literary Forms in the Bible" sidebar on page 13). **Figurative language** uses symbolic images, stories, and names to point to a deeper truth. Figurative language can teach us important religious truths, but it is usually not meant to be scientifically or historically accurate. So, for example, the seven days of creation in chapter 1 of Genesis teach us that God created the world with order and purpose. But we should not interpret this story to mean that God literally created the universe in six twenty-four-hour days. We should also not interpret figurative language as pure fantasy; the first chapters of Genesis affirm real events that took place at the beginning of human history.

Pope Benedict XVI taught that faith and reason support each other. If there seems to be a contradiction between faith and reason, then we have misunderstood one or both of them.

© Alessandra Benedetti/Corbis

Catholic Wisdom

Benedict XVI on Science and Faith

Pope Benedict XVI often taught that science and faith should complement each other:

> Christianity does not posit an inevitable conflict between supernatural faith and scientific progress. The very starting-point of Biblical revelation is the affirmation that God created human beings, endowed them with reason, and set them over all the creatures of the earth. (2006 Address to the Pontifical Academy of Sciences)

Another example is the account in Genesis 2:21 in which God makes the first woman from one of the first man's ribs. Through this text God is revealing that men and women are intimately connected; we are equal, each gender complementing the other. Man and woman are called to be "one flesh" in the Sacrament of Matrimony. But Genesis 2:21 is not trying to teach that God literally made the first woman from a piece of the first man. In trying to "prove" this, some people even say that men have one less rib than women, but, of course, this is not true.

Religious truth and scientific truth will ultimately never contradict each other. God has given us both our faith and our reason, and he would not cause his gifts to us to be in conflict. If religion and science seem to contradict each other, it means that we have misunderstood one or the other. Trying to interpret the figurative language in the Bible as scientific truth is a misunderstanding that causes an unnecessary conflict between our faith and our reason, a conflict God never intended. ☩

Literary Forms in the Bible

Before talking about the meaning of the creation accounts in Sacred Scripture, it is helpful to understand its **literary form.** This is also called the literary genre. A newspaper, for example, has many literary forms: news stories, editorial opinions, comics, advice columns, box scores, and many others. They all can teach us something true, but we don't interpret a comic strip the same way we interpret a front-page news story.

God did not take away the creativity of the human authors as they wrote the books that would eventually become Sacred Scripture. So Sacred Scripture also has many literary forms. The figurative language in Genesis, chapters 1–11, is one kind of literary form. But Sacred Scripture also contains hymns, parables, short stories, law codes, hero stories, prophetic oracles, Gospels, letters, proverbs, religious histories, and even love poetry. How many of these can you find in the Bible?

God works through all these different literary forms to reveal his truth. To interpret the Bible's truth correctly, we must take into account what the human authors intended to communicate through the literary forms they used.

Article 2 Creation Reflects the Glory of God

© Stephen Strathdee/iStockphoto.com

Human beings have experienced a particular kind of awe-inspiring moment throughout all of history. A group of people is returning home from a hunting expedition or from tending their flock or from a well-played game at a neighboring school. They gaze into the evening sky as they travel. The clouds are tinged with beautiful shades of red and purple, and the setting sun reflects golden rays off the land. "Praise God" or maybe even "Yeah, God!" someone says, a recognition that creation itself gives glory to the Creator. God created the world to reveal his glory. Every creature is meant to share in God's truth, goodness, and beauty.

Praise the LORD from the heavens;
    give praise in the heights.
Praise him, all you angels;
    give praise, all you hosts.
Praise him, sun and moon;
    give praise, all shining stars.
. . . .
Young men and women too,
    old and young alike.
Let them all praise the LORD's name,
    for his name alone is exalted,
        majestic above earth and heaven.
                    (Psalm 148:1–3,12–13)

© Erich Lessing/Art Resource, NY

This image of God creating the sun and the moon is from a famous mural painted by Michelangelo in the Sistine Chapel of the Vatican.

Creation: The Work of the Three-In-One

The Scriptures joyfully proclaim that creation is evidence for the power of God. There are those who say the opposite and claim that creation simply happened, that there is no divine Creator. But faith and reason lead us to the sure knowledge that there is one God who created the universe and continues to sustain it through his love. He exists outside of space and time. Or maybe more accurately, space and time are the creation of God.

Sometimes Christians mistakenly believe that creation is the work of only God the Father. The Scriptures testify that creation is the work of all three Persons of the Trinity: Father, Son, and Holy Spirit. The role of Jesus Christ, the Word of God and the Second Person of the Trinity, is explicitly mentioned at the beginning of the Gospel of John:

> In the beginning was the Word,
>   and the Word was with God,
>   and the Word was God.
> He was in the beginning with God.
> All things came to be through him,
>   and without him, nothing came to be.
>   (1:1–3)

The involvement of the Holy Spirit, the Third Person of the Trinity, is a bit more hidden. The opening of Genesis says "a mighty wind swept over the waters" (1:2) of the abyss but this can also be translated "the spirit of God" was over the waters, because in Hebrew the word *ruah* means "breath," "wind," and "spirit." You might also take a look at Psalm 33:6 and notice that it too says that the Lord created the heavens by his word (Jesus Christ) and his breath (Holy Spirit). Sacred Tradition makes it clear that Bible passages like these teach us that creation is the work of all three Divine Persons of the Holy Trinity. God and God alone freely created the universe without help from anyone or anything.

Creation Seen and Unseen

In the time we live in, people put a lot of emphasis on science. This means we tend to believe in things we can observe through our five senses. But the Scriptures and **Tradition** teach that part of God's creation includes things

Tradition
This word (from the Latin *traditio*, meaning "to hand on") refers to the process of passing on the Gospel message. Tradition, which began with the oral communication of the Gospel by the Apostles, was written down in the Scriptures, is handed down and lived out in the life of the Church, and is interpreted by the Magisterium under the guidance of the Holy Spirit.

unseen too. We profess our belief in this every time we say the Nicene Creed, which begins, "I believe in one God, the Father, almighty, maker of heaven and earth, of all things visible and invisible." The unseen creation, which we usually call the spiritual, is every bit as real as the visible reality, which we call the earthly realm.

So what creatures exist in the heavenly realm? **Angels.** Angels are witnessed to in both the Scriptures and Tradition. They are spiritual beings who are the servants and messengers of God. They are present throughout all of salvation history and appear to human beings at key moments. For example, an angel stops Abraham from sacrificing Isaac (see

Angels in the Scriptures

Here's a list of the three angels the Bible mentions by name and the two it mentions by type:

Angel	Biblical Appearances
Raphael	Raphael appears in the Book of Tobit. He is a companion and protector of Tobiah.
Gabriel	Gabriel appears to Daniel and explains the meaning of Daniel's visions (see Daniel 8:16, 9:21). He also appears to Zechariah and Mary in the Gospel of Luke (see 1:19,26).
Michael	In the Book of Daniel, Michael is revealed as the protector of Israel (see 10:21, 12:1). He is also mentioned in the Book of Jude (see verse 9), and he is identified as the archangel who leads the fight against Satan in the Book of Revelation (see 12:7).
Cherubim	These angels were close to God, directly serving him. Images of them adorned the Ark of the Covenant (see Exodus, chapter 25) and Solomon's Temple (see 1 Kings, chapter 6). They appeared in the prophet Ezekiel's visions (see chapter 10)
Seraphim	These angels are mentioned in Isaiah, chapter 6. Their purpose seems to be to serve God and proclaim his glory.

Genesis 22:11–12). An angel announces to Joseph and Mary the birth of Jesus (see Matthew 1:20 and Luke 1:26–27). Angels announce the Resurrection of Christ (see Matthew 28:2–7). The angels glorify God without ceasing, and in Heaven we will join our voices with theirs in praising and glorifying God (see Revelation 5:11). ✝

angel

Based on a word meaning "messenger," a personal and immortal creature with intelligence and free will who constantly glorifies God and serves as a messenger of God to humans to carry out God's saving plan.

soul

Our spiritual principle, it is immortal, and it is what makes us most like God. Our soul is created by God. It is the seat of human consciousness and freedom.

Article

3 Human Beings: The Summit of Creation

As we continue our exploration of God's plan, we face a critical question: Do human beings have a special role, a special place in God's plan? Some people would answer this question by saying we are just the same as all the other animals; we are just a more highly evolved form of life with greater intelligence. So human life has no meaning other than what we give it. These people are wrong, however well-intentioned they might be. God has revealed that humanity indeed has a unique role, a very special place, in his plan.

Once again we turn to the creation account in Genesis. "God created man in his image; / in the divine image he created him; / male and female he created them" (1:27). No other living being is created in God's image. We are the only creature God created with a body and an immortal **soul**. Our soul, created by God, is our spiritual principle. It is what makes us most like God. The union of our body and soul is so complete that we cannot distinguish or separate one from another until our death. At our death our soul will live on until it is reunited once again with our resurrected body.

Male and Female

You might have noticed the phrase "male and female he created them" in the quotation from Genesis. Because this verse has the form of Hebrew poetry, each line is a different way of saying the same thing. The biblical author is telling us that both sexes are made in the image of God. God created men and women to be of equal dignity, yet with distinct characteristics. Both maleness and femaleness reflect God's infinite perfection.

God created men and women for each other. "The LORD God said: 'It is not good for the man to be alone. I will make a suitable partner for him'" (Genesis 2:18). The Genesis account makes it clear that we are not meant to be solitary creatures. God created us to be in communion with each other, a partnership in which we bring our unique gifts as men and women together. The loving relationship between a man and a woman is the first form of communion between persons, reflecting the perfect communion of the Father, the Son, and the Holy Spirit. In the union of a man and a woman in Marriage, God even shares with us his creative power to bring new life into the world!

Notice the symmetry in this image of Adam and Eve. What does this communicate about Adam and Eve's relationship?

© Imagezoo/Images.com/Corbis

Humanity's Role

It follows by reason that if human beings are unique among God's creatures, then we would have a unique role in his plan. Your grandparents might have used the *Baltimore Catechism* to learn about the Catholic faith when they were growing up. In a very famous answer, it said that "God made us to know him, to love him, and to serve him in this world, and to be happy with him forever in the next." Another way to say this is that humanity's unique role in God's plan has two dimensions: (1) to be in communion with God and to respond to his love by loving him in return, and (2) to serve him, particularly as stewards of his creation. Let's take a closer look at each of these dimensions.

Of all God's creatures, we are the only ones who can freely choose to return his love, to choose to share in his own life. God has given us free will and self-knowledge. Because of this we have a dignity that surpasses all other creatures. We are not just something, we are someone!

The greatest testimony to human dignity is the Incarnation. From the beginning, humanity has been destined to "reproduce the image of God's Son made man, 'the image of the invisible God' (Colossians 1:15)" (*Catechism of the Catholic Church [CCC]*, 381). When the fullness of human dignity was lost through Original Sin, God put in motion a plan to restore what we had lost. When the time was right, the Son of God assumed our human nature, restoring the fullness of human dignity. Jesus Christ, true God and true man, became the firstborn of God's sons and daughters. Through Baptism we are his brothers and sisters, sons and daughters of God.

Live It!

Be Who God Created You to Be

It could be said that the hardest challenge in life is to be who God created you to be. We're not talking about whether you should be a postal carrier, a doctor, a priest, or a carpenter. We are talking about believing that you and every person you meet are made in the image and likeness of God. This means treating yourself and every person the same way you would treat Jesus Christ.

Wouldn't it be a perfect world if everyone lived like this? It would be a world in which everyone was patient, kind, polite, unselfish, and slow to anger (see 1 Corinthians, chapter 13). Well, guess what? The seed and the beginning of this world is already here. We call it the Kingdom of God. The Father sent his Son, Jesus Christ, who announced the Kingdom of God and made it present through his life, suffering, death, and Resurrection. The Holy Spirit empowers us to live it. So what do you need to do to truly be the person God created you to be? How will you show that you believe that every person, especially those that are hard for you to love, is made in the image of God?

Humanity's Responsibility

The creation account in Genesis summarizes the second dimension of humanity's unique role in God's plan: "God blessed them, saying to them: 'Be fertile and multiply; fill the earth and subdue it. Have dominion over the fish of the sea, the birds of the air, and all the living things that move on the earth'" (1:28). This passage teaches us that God has given human beings all the other creatures for our benefit. He has put the earth and everything that lives on it in our care.

God willed the great diversity of creatures that exists into being. Each living thing has its own goodness and own unique place in creation. Further, there is an order and interdependence among all creatures. Science has discovered how complex these relationships are in the plant and animal world. The removal of just one species can threaten a whole ecosystem. And God has given us the responsibility for nurturing his creation. We must respect each creature's goodness and place in the order of creation. We are called to care for the earth until the time Christ returns and brings about "a new heaven and a new earth" (Revelation 21:1). ✝

These people are rescuing animals from an oil spill. How would you rate humanity's care of the earth in recent years?

© Natalie Fobes/Science Faction/Corbis

Article 4 The Garden of Eden: The Perfect Life

How would you describe the perfect life? Can you even imagine what such a life would be like? Would you be on a tropical island, with perfect weather every day, with delicious food nearby just waiting to be picked and eaten? Well, one man and woman did have a perfect life, at least at first. Adam and Eve started out not only in a perfect place, the Garden of Eden, but also in perfect relationship with God and each other.

Original Holiness and Original Justice

Adam and Eve appear in Genesis 2:4—3:24. As was previously discussed, this account was written in figurative or symbolic language, so the elements must be interpreted symbolically (see "Symbolic Elements in the Biblical Account of Adam and Eve" sidebar).

As you read about Adam and Eve, it is important to focus on the quality of the relationships. First notice the relationship between Adam and God. God breathes his life directly into Adam, a very intimate act. God walks in

Pray It!

Prayers for Creation Stewardship

In God's plan he gave the care of all creation to human beings. In the Church's liturgy, we ask for God's help in caring for the earth. This is the opening prayer for the Mass for the Blessing of Human Labor:

O God, who willed to subject
the forces of nature to human labor,
mercifully grant
that, undertaking in a Christian spirit what we are to do,
we may merit to join our brothers and sisters
in practicing sincere charity
and in advancing the fulfillment of your divine work of creation.
(Roman Missal)

There is a great deal of evidence that human beings have not been very good stewards of this gift. This is why it is important in our own personal prayer to ask the Holy Spirit for wisdom to guide us in making good choices to care for creation. It is God's creation, and we are privileged to share in its care!

original holiness
The original state of human beings in their relationship with God, sharing in the divine life in full communion with him.

anthropomorphic
Attributing human characteristics to something that is not human.

original justice
The state of complete harmony of our first parents with themselves, with each other, and with all of creation.

the garden, talking to Adam as a friend. He is concerned for Adam's happiness and works to make the perfect partner for Adam. All of this is a symbolic way of saying that God intended the first human beings to share in his life, to be in direct communion with him. We call this state **original holiness.**

In this Scripture account, the human author of Genesis is describing God **anthropomorphically,** meaning God is depicted in a human way. This technique relies on the use of analogy—that is, it describes God as being like a human being and with human characteristics. We must of course, understand that this analogy, like any description of God, is imperfect. "Our human words always fall short of the mystery of God" (*CCC*, 42). However, by describing him with human characteristics the biblical author emphasizes God's closeness to Adam and Eve.

Next notice the relationship between Adam and Eve and their relationship with the rest of creation. Adam and Eve were of one mind and one body, a relationship symbolized by the fact that Eve was made from a part of Adam. Their feeling no shame in each other's presence, even though they were naked, symbolizes their complete honesty and respect for each other. At the beginning their work in caring for the garden and producing food was not a burden. This symbolizes their harmony with the rest of creation. This state of complete harmony between Adam and Eve and the rest of creation is called **original justice.**

The artist who created this painting is trying to convey the Garden of Eden before the Fall. How would you describe what is being portrayed?

Symbolic Elements in the Biblical Account of Adam and Eve

Symbol	Meaning
Adam	A word that in Hebrew means "human being." It is a symbolic name for the first man created by God.
Eve	A word that in Hebrew sounds like "living." It is a symbolic name for the first woman created by God, the mother of all the living.
Garden of Eden	*Eden* sounds like a Hebrew word meaning "delight." So it is a garden of delight, a paradise.
God's blowing the breath of life into Adam	In biblical times breath was considered the source of life. So by blowing into the man made of clay, God is sharing his divine life with the first human beings.
God's creating animals for Adam	In the first creation account, human beings are the last thing God makes, symbolizing that we are the height of God's creative work. But in the second creation account, human beings are made first, symbolizing that all the creatures of the world are made for the delight of humanity.
God's making Eve from Adam's rib	Making the first woman from a piece of the first man is a symbol of the closeness and unity that is to exist between man and woman, particularly in Marriage.
Serpent	The serpent was considered an unclean animal because it moved on the ground without feet. It was also a symbol of the Canaanite goddess Asherah. So it was a symbol of something unclean and deceitful and eventually is identified with Satan.

The state of original holiness and justice is God's will, his plan for all humanity. God wants us to be happy. That happiness comes from our friendship and full communion with God, with other people, and with creation. Even though this plan was interrupted, God's will is not blocked. Those with faith in God—the Father, Son, and Holy Spirit—will experience a taste of original holiness and justice in this life and will know it completely in Heaven. ✟

Part Review

1. Explain what is meant by *primeval history*. Where do you find this in the Bible?

2. Give two examples of the use of figurative or symbolic language in the first eleven chapters of Genesis.

3. What is the relationship between creation and the Trinity?

4. What are angels and what do they do?

5. Give a theological definition of the word *soul*.

6. Give one or two reasons why God created two genders.

7. What is original holiness? What is original justice?

Part 2

The Fall from Grace

God has a plan for us, but our first parents, Adam and Eve, decided not to cooperate with the plan. They disobeyed God's direct command, and this sin resulted in an event called the Fall. The Fall is Adam and Eve's fall from their state of original holiness and justice. The result is that every person born since Adam and Eve is born with Original Sin. Original Sin deprives us of our original holiness and justice and is a wound in our relationship with God. It weakens our ability to resist temptation, making it easier for us to commit sin.

A key character in the account of the Fall is the serpent, the deceiver. The Scriptures and Tradition identify the serpent as Satan, a fallen angel who is opposed to God. Satan and the other fallen angels rejected God completely. Now Satan tempts others to do the same. But God's power is infinite, and his saving plan will prevail over the power of Satan and evil.

The topics covered in this part are:

- Article 5: "Adam and Eve's Disobedience" (page 26)

- Article 6: "Original Sin: A Consequence of the Fall" (page 29)

- Article 7: "Satan and the Fallen Angels" (page 31)

Article 5 Adam and Eve's Disobedience

In his Letter to the Romans, Saint Paul says: "What I do, I do not understand. For I do not do what I want, but I do what I hate" (7:15). He is describing an experience that all people since Adam and Eve have had, with the exception of Jesus Christ and his Mother, Mary. You have probably had this experience. We sin even when we know it is wrong. We make choices to hurt others, and even ourselves, for very selfish reasons. People who have serious addictions struggle with this experience every day. Why would God make us like this? Well, he didn't exactly. The attractiveness of sin and the many ways we delude ourselves into thinking sin is okay are, to a large degree, results of the sin of our first parents.

The Fall

We now come to a truly tragic moment in God's plan. We must take a closer look at the second part of the symbolic account of Adam and Eve (see Genesis 3:1–24). You are probably familiar with this passage, but read it over again. Earlier God gives Adam and Eve only one command: "You are free to eat from any of the trees of the garden except for the tree of knowledge of good and bad. From that tree you shall not eat; the moment you eat from it you are surely doomed to die" (2:16–17). Then the serpent comes along and basically tells Eve the exact opposite. And Eve eats the forbidden fruit and gives it to Adam, who does the same.

Why are Adam and Eve trying to conceal themselves in this image? What does this teach us about sin?

© Rodger, Willie/Private Collection/The Bridgeman Art Library

Immediately Adam and Eve realize they are naked, which is a symbolic way of saying they feel guilt and shame. They are experiencing two feelings God did not intend humans to know. They are ashamed to be seen by each other (the reason for the fig leaves) and ashamed to be seen by God (the reason they hide from him). When God confronts them about their disobedience, they play the blame game. Adam blames Eve for his sin, and Eve blames the serpent. In their shame they cannot be honest with God and accept responsibility for their actions.

All of this—the shame at their nakedness, their hiding from God, their blaming others for their choices—is a symbolic way of saying that Adam and Eve have lost their original holiness and justice. They are no longer in loving communion with God, nor are they in harmony with each other. They must leave the Garden of Eden; they no longer live in paradise. And their disobedience will affect the future of all humanity. No other human beings will be conceived with their holiness and justice intact. This is why it is now harder for us to do what we should do and easier to do what we hate. **The Fall** of Adam and Eve is the origin and the result of Original Sin, a topic covered more in depth in the next article.

Fall, the
Also called the Fall from grace, the biblical Revelation about the origins of sin and evil in the world, expressed figuratively in the account of Adam and Eve in Genesis.

What Was the Sin?

You might wonder exactly what Adam and Eve's sin was. Yes, they disobeyed God's command, but why would God not want them to eat from the tree of knowledge of good and bad (or evil)? Wouldn't having that knowledge be a good thing? To understand this we must consider the culture of the time and the use of figurative language. For the sacred author of Genesis, the full knowledge of good and evil belongs to God alone, who is the source of everything. So the tree symbolizes what human beings can never be: God

Live It!

Facing Temptation

Most people do not intend to do evil things. We are most often tempted when something sinful looks or feels good to us. In the Lord's Prayer, we ask God to "lead us not into temptation." We are asking God to keep us out of tempting situations and to help us not give in to temptations that cross our path.

Avoiding temptation completely is impossible. Even Jesus had to face temptation. "The Spirit drove [Jesus] out into the desert, and he remained . . . tempted by Satan" (Mark 1:12–13). With God's help we can face our temptations and see them for what they are: evil disguised as good. Next time you are tempted, think about what would happen if you gave in to it. What would happen the next day? the next month? years from now? How would it affect you? your friends? your family? What are the false promises? the real consequences?

etiology
A story that explains
something's cause or
origin.

himself. Eating the fruit from that tree is a symbolic way of saying, "We don't need God; we can be gods ourselves." The tragic irony is that God had already given Adam and Eve the greatest gift possible: they are made in God's image (see 1:27) and they have the grace of full communion with God. Seduced by the serpent's lie, "you will be like gods" (3:5), they ended up losing the grace of original holiness and justice. Their sin was a misuse of human freedom and a lack of trust in God. They did not accept the gift of their humanity and instead tried to replace God with themselves. In some way these two things—not accepting our own goodness and a lack of trust in God—are at the root of every sin. ✝

Biblical Etiologies

After the Fall, God describes the consequences for Adam and Eve and the serpent. This list is a literary type called an **etiology.** An etiology is a story that explains something's cause or origin. Genesis 3:14–19 gives the answers to a number of questions ancient people had:

- Why are snakes shunned by other animals?
- Why don't snakes have legs?
- Why is childbirth so painful?
- Why is it so hard for men and women to get along?
- Why is earning a living so much work?
- Why do we have to die?

Today we have scientific explanations for many of these questions. But in symbolic language, this etiology explains the spiritual result of the Fall. Life is now hard, often painful, and we die. Fortunately, God has a plan for restoring us to full communion and it is set into motion even as Adam and Eve experience the consequences of their disobedience.

Article 6 Original Sin: A Consequence of the Fall

Here's an interesting exercise. If you wrote down five doctrines that are essential for understanding Christianity, what would they be? Would Original Sin make your list? (Of course, all the truths of our faith are important. They all fit together and support one another to help us see more clearly God's will and plan for us.) The doctrine of the Trinity is the most essential truth, but without Original Sin there would have been no need for the Son of God to become flesh and live among us. We would all be living in paradise. So we need to understand it. But always remember that sin does not defeat God. As Saint Paul said, "Where sin increased, grace overflowed all the more" (Romans 5:20).

No One Is Exempt

Original Sin is the name for the fact that "Adam and Eve transmitted to their descendants human nature wounded by their own first sin and hence deprived of original holiness and justice" (*CCC*, 417). The Scriptures and Tradition do not explain exactly how this happens. We accept it as a mystery that we cannot fully understand. What we know is that Adam and Eve did not receive their state of original holiness for themselves alone but for all human nature. When they sinned their sin didn't affect just themselves but affected their human nature, which was passed on to all their descendants.

Perhaps this analogy will help you to understand. If for some reason a genetic abnormality develops in a person's DNA—such as nearsightedness—it may get passed on to the person's children. The children didn't do anything to deserve this physical defect, but they still receive it. In a similar way, a defect was created in Adam and Eve's human nature that now gets passed on to all people (with two exceptions: Jesus and his Mother, Mary). We didn't do anything to be in this state; we were born into the state of Original Sin before we ever had a chance to commit a personal sin ourselves!

Original Sin

From the Latin *origo*, meaning "beginning" or "birth." The term has two meanings: (1) the sin of the first human beings, who disobeyed God's command by choosing to follow their own will and so lost their original holiness and became subject to death, (2) the fallen state of human nature that affects every person born into the world.

The Results of Original Sin

concupiscence
The tendency of all human beings toward sin, as a result of Original Sin.

Because of Original Sin, human nature is weakened. The loss of original holiness and justice makes things that should be natural to us harder and more challenging. Relationships with others that should come naturally are marked by tension and misunderstanding. Moral decisions that should be easy and straightforward become more difficult and confused; we are more inclined to sin, an inclination that in the history of the Church is called **concupiscence.** All of this leads to more pain and suffering in our lives.

But there is an even more serious loss because of Original Sin. Our relationship with God is now clouded and hidden. We no longer naturally walk in the garden with God as with a close friend. Even though God desires to be just as close to us as he was to Adam and Eve, we struggle to find him. And the most serious loss of all is that we now experience death. What God had warned Adam about has come true: "From that tree you shall not eat; the moment you eat from it you are surely doomed to die" (Genesis 2:17).

Original Sin does not cause us to lose our goodness or make us completely spiritually corrupt. Some of the Protestant reformers taught that Original Sin had completely perverted human nature and destroyed our freedom to choose right and wrong, and some Protestants today still hold that belief. In response, the Catholic Church more clearly articulated her teaching on God's Revelation. Original Sin does not completely pervert human goodness, but it does weaken our natural powers for relating to God and for choosing to do good.

Catholic Wisdom

Conscience

With the gift of God's grace—the free and undeserved help that he gives us to respond to his call— we are still able to know and do what is good despite our fallen state. The *Pastoral Constitution on the Church in the Modern World* (*Gaudium et Spes,* 1965) reminds us of this:

> In the depths of his conscience, man detects a law which he does not impose upon himself, but which holds him to obedience. Always summoning him to love good and avoid evil, the voice of conscience . . . speaks to his heart: do this, shun that. For man has in his heart a law written by God; to obey it is the very dignity of man. (16)

Death is a consequence of Original Sin but death is not our final end. Jesus Christ has conquered death and opened the gates of Heaven.

© Judi Ashlock/iStockphoto.com

The Spiritual Battle

The doctrine of Original Sin is behind another important concept in the Scriptures and Tradition. The concept is this: since the fall of Adam and Eve, the human race has been involved in a spiritual battle between good and evil. On one side of this battle is Satan, the evil one, who continues to tempt human beings to reject God and God's laws. On the other side of the battle is God—the Father, Son, and Holy Spirit—who has promised to help us win this battle against evil. In fact, Jesus Christ has already won the battle through his Passion, death, Resurrection, and Ascension. We just have to decide whose side we are going to be on! ✝

Satan

The fallen angel or spirit of evil who is the enemy of God and a continuing instigator of temptation and sin in the world.

7 Satan and the Fallen Angels

Article

The deceiving serpent is introduced in the account of the Fall. Tradition identifies the serpent as **Satan.** Satan is a popular character in television, movies, and music. Sometimes he is pictured in demonic form with goat's horns. This image is taken from Matthew 25:31–46 when Jesus separates the sheep, who are going to Heaven, from the goats, who are going to Hell. Sometimes Satan is presented as a smooth-talking, well-dressed, but always deceptive businessman. Both of these images tell us something true about Satan. He is a liar and he is dangerous to our spiritual well-being. The danger with the media portrayal of Satan is if it leads us to believe that he is not real. He is very, very real.

The Origin of the Fallen Angels

The Bible gives us only a hint of the nature of Satan and his demons. The Second Letter of Peter has this passing reference: "God did not spare the angels when they sinned, but condemned them to the chains of Tartarus and handed them over to be kept for judgment" (2:4; see also Jude, chapter 6). This supports what God has revealed through Sacred Tradition. The Devil and his demons are fallen angels. These angels, through their own free choice, totally and completely rejected God and his Reign. Because of this they could no longer be in the presence of God and were cast from Heaven (see Luke 10:18).

The greatest of these fallen angels is Satan, also called the Devil or Lucifer. Satan's identity develops over time in the Scriptures (see "Satan in the Bible" sidebar). By New Testament times, he emerges as God's fierce opponent. Satan is bold enough to tempt Jesus himself at the

© Bildarchiv Preussischer Kulturbesitz/Art Resource, NY

This painting depicts Michael the Archangel in battle against Satan and his demons. Why does the artist depict the demonic forces as very bestial?

beginning of Christ's ministry (see Luke 4:1–11). The Devil is even partially responsible for the death of Christ, entering Judas before he betrays Christ (see John 13:27). Early Christians are warned to be on the alert for Satan, who is "prowling around like a roaring lion" (1 Peter 5:8) looking to devour the unwary.

Parousia
The second coming of Christ at the end of time, fully realizing God's plan and the glorification of humanity.

Satan's Power Is Limited

As a spiritual force, Satan is powerful, but he is not all-powerful. He has already lost his war with God, and Christians have no reason to fear him. Christ has won the victory over Satan through his death on the cross. Now all that remains is for Satan to be thrown into Hell forever at the Final Judgment (see Revelation 20–21).

As we await the **Parousia,** Satan continues to have the power to tempt us to sin. But he cannot force us to do anything against our will. We have been given grace from the Holy Spirit to resist the Devil's temptations. The pain and suffering in the world caused by human sin may start with Satan's temptations, but the freely made choices of human beings actually cause it. So be on the watch for Satan's temptations, but do not fear him. The power of Christ will protect you from Satan. ✝

Pray It!

Deliver Us from Evil

When thinking of evil, some people often see images of a red creature with horns and a pitchfork. But evil comes in much more real and concrete forms. We sometimes convince ourselves that evil is "out there," perpetrated by other people, but the truth is that we often participate in evil. It is easy to point a finger at the evil carried out by others, but it is extremely painful to admit the evil committed by our own hands.

Jesus taught us to "remove the wooden beam from your eye first; then you will see clearly to remove the splinter from your brother's eye" (Matthew 7:5). Let us prayerfully acknowledge where we have fallen short and ask God to deliver us from . . . gossip . . . cheating . . . addiction . . . greed . . . racism . . . drug abuse . . . bullying . . . pornography . . . hatred . . . abortion . . . lies . . . poverty . . . violence . . . sexual promiscuity . . . selfishness . . . and all the other dark places that lead us away from him.

Satan in the Bible

Surprisingly to some people, in Satan's earliest appearances in the Bible, he is a member of God's heavenly court. In Hebrew *Satan* literally means "adversary." In the Old Testament, he is referenced only three times: Job, chapters 1 and 2, 1 Chronicles 21:1, and Zechariah 3:1–2. In Job and Zechariah, Satan is portrayed as an angel whose role is to point out to God human sinfulness.

The New Testament has lots of references to Satan (who is also called the Devil and Beelzebul). He tempts Jesus in the desert (see Matthew 4:1–11). Jesus calls him "a murderer from the beginning" and "the father of lies" (John 8:44). He is now understood to represent the powers of evil in the world, the leader of a kingdom of darkness (see Mark 3:23–26), and "the prince of demons" (Luke 11:15). Still later he is pictured as the spiritual power behind the empires that persecuted the Israelites and the early Christians. This is particularly evident in the Book of Revelation where Satan is also symbolized as a dragon (see chapters 12–13 and 20). The different images of Satan in the Bible offer another example of why we must consider all of the Scriptures and Tradition when interpreting a specific Bible passage.

Part Review

1. How is the loss of Adam and Eve's original holiness and justice symbolically expressed in Genesis, chapter 3?

2. Explain the deeper meaning of Adam and Eve's sin of disobedience.

3. Who is affected by Original Sin? How are they affected?

4. Describe the spiritual battle that is occurring because of Original Sin.

5. What is the origin of Satan and his demons?

6. What are some of the different ways Satan is described in the Scriptures?

Part 3

The Path to Restoration

God has a plan for us, and it will not be thwarted. After Adam and Eve's Fall from grace, we continue to see God's new plan revealed through the Scriptures and Tradition. He seeks to restore to humanity what was lost in the Fall. This begins with his promise to our first parents. It continues with the Covenants God makes with Noah, Abraham, Moses, and David. Through the Covenant, God establishes his intent to call a Chosen People to be his light for all the nations. He gives them the Law to teach them how to live in right relationship with him and with one other. Unfortunately, we see the continued impact of Original Sin as the Chosen People fail to keep up their end of the Covenant time and time again. And they suffer many terrible consequences because of their lack of faith.

You might think that God would just give up on us. But God's love, patience, and understanding have no human limits. His prophets tirelessly kept warning, directing, and comforting the Chosen People. Their message contained hints at what was to come in God's wonderful plan for our salvation. God would send a Messiah, a chosen one, who would fully restore humanity's original holiness and justice. He would lead with justice, proclaim peace, and as the Suffering Servant, take upon himself all our sins. And the Chosen People began to wait in hope.

The topics covered in this part are:

- Article 8: "God's Promise to Adam and Eve" (page 37)

- Article 9: "The Old Testament Covenants: Part One" (page 41)

- Article 10: "The Old Testament Covenants: Part Two" (page 45)

- Article 11: "Covenant Keeping: Successes and Failures" (page 48)

- Article 12: "The Growing Messianic Hope" (page 53)

Article 8 God's Promise to Adam and Eve

After the Fall things seem pretty bleak for the human race. We have already looked at the consequences of Adam and Eve's sin found in Genesis 3:14–19. Adam and Eve, who are symbolic of all humanity now, have lost God's gifts of original holiness and justice. Their relationships with God, with each other, and with the earth are more difficult and challenging. But hidden in the third chapter of Genesis is a great spiritual truth: even amidst the greatest of tragedies, God does not abandon us. For those who have faith, God will bring good even from sin and suffering.

literal sense
A form of biblical interpretation that considers the explicit meaning of the text. It lays the foundation for all other senses of the Scriptures.

spiritual sense
A form of biblical interpretation that goes beyond the literal sense to consider what the realities and events of the Scriptures signify and mean for salvation.

The *Protoevangelium*

When God delivers the consequences of Adam and Eve's disobedience, he says this to the serpent:

> I will put enmity between you and the woman,
>   and between your offspring and hers;
> He will strike at your head,
>   while you strike at his heel.
>   (Genesis 3:15)

This verse is called the *Protoevangelium*, which is a Latin word meaning "first gospel." The **literal sense** of this verse is that it is an etiology; it explains why snakes and people do not get along very well. But after the experience of Christ's life, death, and Resurrection, the Church Fathers saw a deeper, **spiritual sense** in this verse. They interpreted it as God's first promise to send a Savior to free humanity from

Catholic Wisdom

O Happy Fault!

Can good come out of evil? During the Easter Vigil, the deacon (or a cantor) sings a hymn called the Exultet, which includes the following: O happy fault, that earned so great, so glorious a Redeemer!"

"Happy fault"!? This ironic phrase speaks of the good God gave to us as a result of the sin of the first man and woman. Because humankind was now subject to suffering and sin, God sent his only Son into the world, giving us blessings better than those we had lost.

the effects of the Fall. The following chart will help you to understand their interpretation:

Literal Sign	Spiritual Meaning
the serpent	Satan
the woman	Mary
the woman's offspring	Jesus Christ
enmity between the serpent and the woman, between the serpent and her offspring	the spiritual battle between Satan and God for the future of humanity
"He will strike at your head, while you strike at his heel."	Jesus Christ will win the battle with Satan. A strike at the heel is a position of weakness, but a strike at the head is a death blow.

fratricide
To kill one's own brother or sister.

So even as Adam and Eve are leaving the Garden of Eden, God is already making a promise, a covenant, that he will save humanity from the damage caused by Satan's deception. In this interpretation Mary is the new Eve and Christ is the new Adam. They will restore the original holiness and justice that was lost by Adam and Eve. As the Mother of God, Mary is the first to benefit from Christ's victory over sin. She is conceived without the stain of Original Sin and, with special grace from God, remains free from sin throughout her entire life.

Sin Increases, God Remains Faithful

The accounts that follow the Fall in the primeval history serve two purposes. First, they show the growth and worsening of sin. Second, they show that no matter how bad humanity fell, God remained faithful in finding a way to keep his plan of salvation going.

Cain and Abel (Genesis 4:1–16)

Cain and Abel is a story of jealousy and **fratricide.** Adam and Eve's first two sons, Cain and Abel, are symbols of the two primary ways people fed themselves in biblical times: the shepherds raised animals and the farmers grew crops. Both of them offered the appropriate sacrifice to God. God liked Abel's sacrifice better (because he offered the best of what he raised), and Cain was jealous. He killed Abel. The first sin after the Fall was brother killing brother.

Again, in this account the inspired biblical author is describing God by way of an imperfect analogy that presents God in human terms, as acting in a human manner. First, he tried to warn Cain not to let sin be his master. And after the murder, God marked Cain to prevent anyone from killing him in revenge. God's promise to save the descendants of Adam and Eve is already taking place.

© Stefano Bianchetti/Corbis

Adam and Eve weep over their dead son, Abel. Notice the two altars in the background. The smoke from Abel's sacrifice raises straight up, a symbol that his sacrifice was pleasing to God.

Noah and the Flood (Genesis 6:5—9:17)

The Book of Genesis gives two versions of the generations from Adam to Noah. Humankind has greatly increased in number. And humankind has also greatly increased in sin. God saw how "no desire that [humanity's] heart conceived was ever anything but evil" (6:5). God had no choice but to begin over again. Fortunately, there was one just man, Noah, and his family. Through Noah and his family, God is able to continue his promise to save the descendants of Adam and Eve. But God goes one step further this time. He makes an explicit Covenant or promise with Noah and through Noah with all humankind and all creation: "Never again shall all bodily creatures be destroyed by the waters of a flood" (9:11). God marked this promise with a rainbow. God has committed to saving humanity by some different means than by destroying all sinners. His plan continues to be revealed.

We Gained More Than We Lost

Saint Leo the Great served as Pope from 440–461. These were especially trying times, and Leo protected the Church from a number of heresies. He was a great theologian and homilist and in 1754 was declared a Doctor of the Church. Leo expressed the wonder and joy of the great mystery of God's plan of salvation in one of his sermons:

SAINT LEO
THE GREAT
OF ROME

"For today not only are we confirmed as possessors of paradise, but have also in Christ penetrated the heights of heaven, and have gained still greater things through Christ's unspeakable grace than we had lost through the devil's malice. For us, whom our virulent enemy had driven out from the bliss of our first abode, the Son of God has made members of Himself and placed at the right hand of the Father, with Whom He lives and reigns in the unity of the Holy Spirit, God forever and ever. Amen." (Sermon 73)

The Tower of Babel (Genesis 11:1–9)

Babel is another spelling of *Babylon,* the nation and city where the Israelite leaders were brought as captives. The Babylonians, or more likely their slaves, built tall towers called ziggurats that were the center of politics and religion. During **the Exile,** the Israelites would have remembered these as places of idolatry, the worship of false gods. So the account of the tower of Babel tells about people who tried to make themselves like gods and made god in their own image, something the Israelites had firsthand experience of. Keeping his promise not to destroy all the sinful people with a natural disaster, God instead makes them speak different languages so they cannot understand one another (another etiology). Once again God takes action to keep his plan of salvation in motion.

But something more is needed. Humanity is simply not learning how to be faithful to God. So God will take a more direct approach in his saving plan as the Book of Genesis continues. ✝

Exile, the
The period of the Israelite captivity in Babylon after the destruction of Jerusalem in 587 BC.

Paschal Mystery
The work of salvation accomplished by Jesus Christ mainly through his life, Passion, death, Resurrection, and Ascension.

Article 9 The Old Testament Covenants: Part One

A covenant is a solemn agreement between two parties. Among the nations surrounding ancient Israel, covenants were usually made between two kings, outlining the responsibilities the kings had toward each other. Often the stronger king promised to protect the weaker king, and the weaker king promised to pay tribute or taxes to the more powerful king. But we do not have any records of these kingdoms' having covenants with their gods or goddesses. In their mythology, their deities would never humble themselves to enter into a binding agreement with human beings.

This makes Israel unique. Their covenants are not with other kingdoms but with God. God initiates these covenants and stays faithful to them. Through them he communicates the love he has for humanity and his desire to restore our communion with him. These covenants point us to the **Paschal Mystery,** the redemption of all humanity through Christ's Passion, death, Resurrection, and Ascension. We will look at four of these covenants—those with Noah, Abraham, Moses, and David.

polytheism

The belief in many gods.

The Covenant with Noah

The covenant God made with Noah, and through Noah with the whole human race, was introduced in the previous article. One more thing to consider about this covenant is its universal nature. Directly after God makes this covenant, chapter 10 of Genesis gives a description of how Noah's descendants multiplied to become all the nations of the world: "These are the groupings of Noah's sons, according to their origins and by their nations. From these the other nations of the earth branched out after the flood" (verse 32). This was a way of saying that God's covenant with Noah now extended to all the nations of the earth and will remain in force as long as the world lasts.

However, because of sin these nations are always in danger of **polytheism,** which is the false belief in many gods. They are also always in danger of worshipping their nation and their king instead of God, which is another form of idolatry. Yet the covenant with Noah assures us that God is still at work among these nations. The Bible lifts up several non-Jewish leaders as examples of God's working through other peoples (see the "God-Fearing Gentiles in the Old Testament" sidebar). The covenant with Noah will find its fulfillment in the New Covenant that Jesus Christ extends to all the people of the world.

© PHOTOCREO Michal Bednarek/Shutterstock.com

The rainbow was God's sign to Noah of his love for humanity and his promise to save us.

The Abrahamic Covenant

In chapter 12 of Genesis, the story of Abraham begins. Starting with Abraham, God begins a new phase of his plan to restore humanity's holiness and justice. He does this by calling a Chosen People to be in a unique relationship with him. These people will have a special role in his plan. God establishes this special relationship and its purpose in the

God-Fearing Gentiles in the Old Testament

The Old Testament names several Gentiles, or non-Jews, who were instrumental in God's plan of salvation. The following chart lists the most prominent ones:

Name	Importance
Melchizedek	The king of Salem and a "priest of the Most High" (Genesis 14:18). With Abraham he offered bread and wine in thanksgiving after a successful battle.
Rahab	A Canaanite woman who risked her life to help protect Joshua's spies in the city of Jericho (Joshua 2:1–21).
King Cyrus	The Persian emperor who conquered Babylon and ended the Jewish Exile (see Ezra 1:1–4). He allowed the Judean slaves to return home and even helped to fund the reconstruction of Jerusalem (see 3:7).
Ruth	A Moabite woman who married an Israelite man. She is remembered for her trust in God and her commitment to her Jewish mother-in-law.

Covenant he makes with Abraham. There are several places where God announces his Covenant to Abraham: 12:1–3, 13:14–17, 15:1–19, and 17:1–27. But the later announcements are, for the most part, further elaborations on the Covenant first made in chapter 12, verses 2–6:

> I will make of you a great nation,
>   and I will bless you;
> I will make your name great,
>   so that you will be a blessing.
> I will bless those who bless you
>   and curse those who curse you.
> All the communities of the earth
>   shall find blessing in you.

In his Covenant with Abraham, God promises Abraham three things: (1) to make of him a great nation by promising Abraham many descendants, (2) to provide Abraham and his descendants a land of their own, and (3) to make Abraham and his descendants a blessing for all the nations.

The third promise is the most important one in God's saving plan. The first two promises are the necessary preconditions in order for the third promise to be fulfilled. God's plan is for Abraham's descendants, who will later be called Hebrews, Israelites, and finally Jews, to be an example to all other people of how to live in right relationship with the one, true God. God asks Abraham and his descendants to commit to these things: (1) to walk with God—that is, to recognize the one, true God (see Genesis 17:1), (2) to be blameless—that is to live a life without sin (see 17:1), and (3) to practice **circumcision** as a physical mark of the Covenant (see 17:9–14).

Abraham and his descendants—Isaac and Jacob (whom God renames Israel)—are called the **patriarchs,** and they are revered as saints in the Church's liturgical tradition. The remaining chapters of Genesis tell of how they escape many dangerous situations. Their stories show that God is faithful in keeping his Covenant despite human sin and weakness. Original Sin continues to have its effect. The Israelites will come to worship false gods and goddesses and will be guilty of a variety of sins. This is explored more in a later article. But God remains faithful and his will cannot be overcome by human sin and weakness. God's Covenant with Abraham prepares the way for the coming of the Messiah, Jesus Christ, in whom the Covenant is fulfilled. Through Jesus Christ, a descendant of Abraham, God's blessing is brought to all the nations. ✝

Abraham is a gracious host to his divine visitors. Notice how he kneels before them in the foreground and serves them at a table in the background.

Article 10 The Old Testament Covenants: Part Two

In this article we continue looking at the covenants God made with various people in the Old Testament. Through these covenants God was establishing a Chosen People, a people who are our ancestors in faith. We find this explicitly described in the Book of Deuteronomy, which portrays Moses' final speech to the Israelites. He tells the Israelites that they are "a people sacred to the LORD, your God; he has chosen you from all the nations on the face of the earth to be a people peculiarly his own. It was not because you are the largest of all nations that the LORD set his heart on you. . . . It was because the LORD loved you and because of his fidelity to the oath he had sworn to your fathers" (7:6–7).

The Mosaic Covenant

The most awe-inspiring event in the Old Testament is the **theophany** at Mount Sinai, which is described in Exodus 19:16–25. The Israelites have escaped from Egypt because of God's miraculous intervention and have been journeying for three months. They have come to the Sinai desert and camp at the base of a large mountain. On the third day after their arrival at the mountain, the air is filled with lightning and thunder, the ground shakes, and smoke and fire appear on the mountaintop. These dramatic signs of God's presence are meant to call attention to the critical importance of what comes next.

God summons Moses to the mountaintop and renews with Moses the Covenant he made with Abraham. And he gives Moses a set of laws that the Israelites must follow as their part of the Covenant. This Law is summarized in the Ten Commandments (see Exodus 20:1–17), but the full Law is spelled out in the rest of Exodus and Leviticus. It is summarized again in Deuteronomy. This Law is also called the Mosaic Law or the Old Law. It is old not in the sense of being obsolete, but it is old in the sense that it has been fulfilled in Jesus Christ who is the New Law.

From this point on, the Covenant and the Law are so closely linked that they are understood to be two sides of the same coin. Keeping the Law is the most important sign of faithfulness to the Covenant. Breaking the Law is the same as

circumcision

The act, required by Jewish law, of removing the foreskin of the penis. Since the time of Abraham, it has been a sign of God's Covenant relationship with the Jewish people.

patriarch

The father or leader of a tribe, clan, or tradition. Abraham, Isaac, and Jacob were the patriarchs of the Israelite people.

theophany

God's breaking into the human dimension so an individual's and community's understanding of God is deepened or changed.

Moses receives the Ten Commandments from God to teach the Israelites how to live in right relationship with God and one another. Obeying the Commandments was an important part of the Israelites' Covenant with God.

© David Lees/CORBIS

being unfaithful to the Covenant. The Jewish people eventually call the first five books of their Scriptures—the same five books that begin the Old Testament—the **Torah,** which is the Hebrew word for "law" or "teaching." Through these laws God teaches his Chosen People how to be in right relationship with him and with one another. The Old Law is a step in God's plan for restoring our original holiness and justice. It will become the rule by which the prophets will measure the faithfulness of the kings and the people.

The Davidic Covenant

There is one more promise God makes in the Old Testament that can also be called a covenant. This promise is delivered to King David by the prophet Nathan. David wishes to build a permanent dwelling for the **Ark of the Covenant,** the sacred box in which the tablets with the Ten Commandments are kept. God instructs Nathan to tell David not to build this Temple (see 2 Samuel 7:4–13). Instead David's heir will build it. God then promises David that "your house and your kingdom shall endure forever before me; your throne shall stand firm forever" (verse 16).

In this context a "house" means a bloodline or direct line of descendants. Even though a descendant of David was always ruler of Israel or Judah (the southern kingdom), the kingdom itself was destroyed in 598 BC. After this there were no more Davidic kings. The Gospels help us to understand how this promise was fulfilled. Jesus Christ was a direct descendant of David (see Matthew 1:6, Luke 3:31). Christ established the Kingdom of God, which will endure forever and over which he reigns for eternity. Through him the Covenant with David is fulfilled.

All the Old Testament Covenants are part of God's plan. They assure us of God's loving commitment to humanity. They teach us how to live in right relationship with God and with one another. They point us toward the restoration of our original holiness and justice. But these Covenants by themselves are not enough to bring God's plan of salvation to fulfillment. So they also point the way to something more. That something more is the Messiah, Jesus Christ, whose life, death, Passion, Resurrection, and Ascension—the Paschal Mystery—will bring these ancient Covenants to their final and complete fulfillment. By sending his own Son, God has revealed himself fully to the world. ✝

Torah
A Hebrew word meaning "law," referring to the first five books of the Old Testament.

Ark of the Covenant
A sacred chest that housed the tablets of the Ten Commandments. It was placed within the sanctuary where God would come and dwell.

Pray It!

Frightening Theophanies

When God appears to someone in the movies, it is sometimes presented as a joyous moment. There is a beautiful white light and angels are singing in the background. But in the Bible, more often than not, God's appearances fill those who experience them with fear at encountering the mystery of God. When God established his Covenant with Abraham, "a deep, terrifying darkness enveloped [Abraham]" (Genesis 15:12). Before Moses received the Ten Commandments, Mount Sinai was "wrapped in smoke" and "trembled violently" (Exodus 19:18). It is almost as if it is God's way of saying, "This isn't going to be easy." It is true: our life with God requires courage. Let us pray:

God give me the courage . . .

. . . to be present to you despite my fears

. . . to keep my promises to you even when there are obstacles

. . . to know you are here with me even in the turmoil of my life

. . . to live the New Law taught by and embodied in Jesus Christ, who reminds us that "whoever loses his life for my sake and that of the gospel will save it" (Mark 8:35). Amen.

The Ark of the Covenant

The Ark of the Covenant is described in Exodus 25:10–22. It is to be con-
structed of precious wood and metal to emphasize its sacred purpose. The
tablets containing the Covenant Commandments are to be placed in it. At
the top of the Ark, gold statues of two cherubim (angels who serve God) are
to be placed with their wings creating a seat. The Ark is to be shaped like a
throne, because it will be the seat of God Almighty, King forever.

© The Jewish Museum, NY/Art Resource, NYesource, NY

Article 11 Covenant Keeping: Successes and Failures

The historical books and the writings of the prophets reveal
the Israelites' struggles to keep the Covenant they had made
with God. You have probably covered this history in greater
detail in a previous course. In this article we summarize
three important elements in the Israelites' history: the time
of the judges, the time of the monarchy, and the role of the
prophets.

The Judges of Israel

After the Israelites, led by Joshua, settle in the land of Canaan, they have no central government. They have no king, no high priest, no president. They exist as a **confederation** of tribal groups. When faced with a threat, such as an outside invader, God raises up a hero who rallies one or more tribes in defense of their land. These leaders are called judges, but they are not judges as we have them today. Though they may have settled disputes, they were primarily military leaders. The Book of Judges contains the accounts of twelve of these charismatic leaders, telling about six of them in more detail.

confederation
An alliance of tribes or nations with no central authority.

There is a cycle in Judges related to the Covenant. It would seem that after taking possession of the Promised Land, the Israelites forget the Law and the Covenant again and again. "Abandoning the LORD, the God of their fathers, who had led them out of the land of Egypt, they followed the other gods of the various nations around them, and by their worship of these gods provoked the LORD" (Judges 2:12). God allows them to fall into the hands of their enemies. When they realize their sin and repent and call out to God for deliverance, God raises up a judge to lead the victory against their enemies. Then for a while, the Israelites keep the Covenant before repeating the cycle again.

The Book of Judges shows another step in God's plan of salvation. God wants his Chosen People to be completely committed to him, which they can do by keeping the Law and the Covenant. As long as they do this, they will not need an intermediary, such as a king, to lead them. But they prove incapable of doing this.

© Adriene Cruz/Photo: Art Alexander

Deborah, the only woman judge of Israel, is depicted with her palm tree (see Judges 4:5).

As the period of the Judges continues, even the judges themselves become less exemplary in their behavior. Gideon introduces idolatry (see Judges 8:24–27), Jephthah sacrifices his own daughter (see 11:29–40), and Samson is driven by his own selfish concerns (see chapters 13–16). The period ends with a bloody civil war (see chapter 20). Despite these setbacks God is faithful to the Covenant and does not abandon this seemingly hopeless people.

The Monarchy

Samuel unexpectedly anoints David, the youngest of eight brothers, as the future king of Israel. Why do you think that God's choices are often not what people expect?

The history of the kings of Israel is told in First and Second Samuel and First and Second Kings and is then repeated in First and Second Chronicles. The **monarchy** begins with the Israelites' approaching Samuel, the last judge of Israel, and asking him to appoint a king. Samuel is reluctant to do this because he believes the people are rejecting God as their king. But despite this God directs him to anoint the first king of Israel, Saul (see 1 Samuel, chapter 8). The first three kings

© Art Resource, NY

of Israel are all heroically committed to God and promote the Law and the Covenant. All three are also tragically flawed: Saul with lack of trust, David with lust, and Solomon with greed. Despite their sin and weakness, God works through them to unite the twelve tribes into a strong, united kingdom and eventually to build a Temple in Jerusalem, the center of authentic Israelite worship.

monarchy
A government or a state headed by a single person, like a king or queen. As a biblical term, it refers to the period of time when the Israelites existed as an independent nation.

After Solomon's death, however, the united monarchy is split into two kingdoms, Israel and Judah. The Books of First and Second Kings chronicle the successes and failures of the kings of both kingdoms. The very first king of the northern kingdom (Israel), Jeroboam, gets off to a bad start by setting up idolatrous places of worship. He and the kings who follow him "did evil in the LORD's sight" (1 Kings 15:26). The kings of the southern kingdom (Judah) do not do much better: "Judah did evil in the sight of the LORD, and by their sins angered him even more than their fathers had done" (1 Kings 14:22). But there were good kings of Judah, like Asa, Hezekiah, and Josiah, who brought religious reform and destroyed the places of idolatry and called the people to be faithful again to the Covenant.

As another step in God's plan of salvation, the monarchy firmly establishes the Israelites as God's Chosen People. The practices of religious ritual and worship are established at the Jerusalem Temple. And the great kings, such as David and Solomon, foreshadow the kingship of Jesus Christ. As earthly kingdoms, Israel and Judah do not last. But the noble intention of these Israelite nations—to be kingdoms committed to the Law and the Covenant—will find its fulfillment in the Kingdom of Heaven and the eternal Reign of Jesus Christ.

The Prophets

The Israelite prophets play a key role in relation to the Covenant. In a very real sense, they are the watchdogs of the Covenant and the Law. As God's spokespeople they call the kings and the people to be faithful to the Covenant and warn of the consequences of failing to do so: "Thus says the LORD, the God of Israel: Cursed be the man who does not observe the terms of this covenant, which I enjoined upon your fathers the day I brought them up out of the land of Egypt"

(Jeremiah 11:3–4). But the prophets also assured the people that God would not abandon his Covenant commitment:

> Though the mountains leave their place
> and the hills be shaken,
> My love shall never leave you
> nor my covenant of peace be shaken,
> says the LORD, who has mercy on you.
> (Isaiah 54:10)

The books of the prophets contain the writings of four major prophets—Isaiah, Jeremiah, Ezekiel, and Daniel—and the writings of twelve minor prophets. But there were many more prophets than these who are part of salvation history. These faithful men endured ridicule, torture, and even risked death to speak God's Word. They did this out of love for God's People. They knew that the Israelites' faithfulness to the Covenant was essential for God's plan of salvation. They already were beginning to see that God was planning something big, something new, to complete his plan to redeem all humanity and restore our right relationship with God and with one another (see next article). The prophets foreshadow Christ's own role as prophet, for Jesus Christ will not just proclaim the Word—he is the Word of God made flesh. ✝

Live It!

What Would the Prophets Tell Us?

The prophets of the Old Testament often cried out against the hypocrisy of the Israelites. They pointed out the great gap between the demands of the Covenant (being faithful to God, practicing justice, caring for the poor and needy) and how the Israelites were actually living. For example, Amos tells the people that their worship means nothing to God because they are not living good and just lives. Their prayers have become empty and hollow. Only when they "let justice surge like water, and goodness like an unfailing stream" (Amos 5:24) will their worship have any meaning again. Today the words of the prophets remind us to be faithful to the teachings of Christ by becoming peacemakers, caring for the poor, and loving those who we do not like. Our worship on Sunday is most authentic when we are faithful to Christ's teachings. "Faith . . . if it does not have works, is dead" (James 2:17).

Article 12 The Growing Messianic Hope

Hope. It is an important virtue and a gift of faith. Hope creates in us a desire and an expectation for our salvation and the Kingdom of God. The prophets were God's instruments of hope to his Chosen People. He revealed to the prophets a vision of a New Covenant and a new heavenly kingdom. This would be brought about through the work of a messiah, which literally means "anointed one."

> "A child is born to us, a son is given us."
> (Isaiah 9:5)

By proclaiming this vision, the prophets gave the Chosen People hope for a future in which humanity's relationship with God would be fully restored. In the centuries preceding the birth of Christ, many faithful Jews waited in expectant hope for this promised Messiah who would deliver them from their earthly and spiritual bondage. Their wait was over when Jesus Christ, the only begotten Son of the Father, was conceived by the power of the Holy Spirit and born of the Virgin Mary. The chart on page 54 outlines some of the more important prophecies of hope proclaimed by the prophets. ✝

On Christian Hope

Pope Benedict XVI's second encyclical letter specifically addressed Christian hope. In this beautiful letter, he outlined the importance of the virtue of hope in the life of the believer. The Pope's letter began as follows:

According to the Christian faith, "redemption"—salvation—is not simply a given. Redemption is offered to us in the sense that we have been given hope, trustworthy hope, by virtue of which we can face our present: the present, even if it is arduous, can be lived and accepted if it leads towards a goal, if we can be sure of this goal, and if this goal is great enough to justify the effort of the journey. (*Spe Salvi*, 1)

You can easily find Pope Benedict XVI's encyclical online. It is enlightening and inspiring reading.

Some Important Prophecies of Hope

Location	Description	Connection to Christ
Isaiah 9:1–6	Isaiah prophesies that the "people who walked in darkness have seen a great light." A child will be born to lead them and among his names will be "God-Hero" and "Prince of Peace." His kingdom will be just and peaceful forever.	Jesus Christ is the Prince of Peace and the Son of God who forever rules the Kingdom of Heaven.
Isaiah 11:1–9	Isaiah prophesies about a coming ruler from the "stump of Jesse." He shall "judge the poor with justice" and "with the breath of his lips he shall slay the wicked." Even natural enemies will play together peacefully in his kingdom.	Jesus Christ is a descendant of Jesse (David's father).
Isaiah 52:13—53:12	This is one of the suffering servant passages in Isaiah. Isaiah prophesies of a servant of the Lord who is "smitten for the sin of his people." "The LORD laid upon him the guilt of us all" and "by his stripes we were healed."	This prophecy is an uncannily accurate description of Christ's Passion. He suffered and died for our salvation.
Jeremiah 31:31–34	Jeremiah prophesies about a new covenant God will make with Israel and Judah: "I will place my law within them, and write it upon their hearts."	The New Covenant is established in Jesus Christ. Through the power of the Holy Spirit, Christ lives in every believer's heart.
Ezekiel 34:11–31	Ezekiel prophesies that God will act like a good shepherd, rescuing his People, giving them safe pasture, and healing their injuries. He will "make a covenant of peace with them" and "free them from the power of those who enslaved them."	In the Gospel of John, Christ declares that he is the Good Shepherd.
Ezekiel 37:1–14	Ezekiel has a vision of a valley of dry bones being resurrected and coming alive again. "O my people, I will open your graves and have you rise from them."	With the coming of the New Covenant, all the faithful who have died will rise again, having been saved through the Passion, death, and Resurrection of Jesus Christ.
Zechariah 9:9–10	Zechariah prophesies about a king and a "just savior." He shall "proclaim peace to the nations" and "his dominion shall be from sea to sea."	Jesus Christ is the promised King and just Savior.

Part Review

1. Give an interpretation of the *Protoevangelium* using both the literal and spiritual senses of the passage.

2. How do the accounts of Cain and Abel and Noah and the Flood explain the effects of Original Sin and also God's promise of salvation?

3. How is God's Covenant with Noah different from his Covenant with Abraham?

4. What does God promise in his Covenant with Abraham?

5. Explain the connection between the Mosaic Covenant and the Mosaic Law.

6. How is God's promise to David fulfilled?

7. Describe two Old Testament prophecies of hope and how they are fulfilled in Jesus Christ.

Jesus Christ's Mission Is Revealed

Part 1

The Word Became Flesh

God has a plan, and it is important that you are familiar with it. In the previous section, we studied how God took patient steps to call and prepare his Chosen People. But despite God's gifts of the Covenant and the prophets, his Chosen People could not maintain their faithfulness. In this section we study how God's plan to offer redemption to all humanity is brought to fulfillment. The angel's announcement to Mary that she will bear the Son of God is the beginning of what Saint Paul calls "the fullness of time" (Galatians 4:4). Through the power of the Holy Spirit, Mary will conceive a son and name him Jesus, meaning "God saves." Mary becomes the Mother of God and is supported by Joseph, her husband and Jesus' human foster father.

This great mystery, that the Eternal Son of God assumed a human nature in order to save us, had been foreshadowed through God's relationship with his Chosen People. In recognition of this, the sacred writers of the New Testament showed how many of the Old Testament prophecies applied to Jesus. They made clear that in obedience to his Father, Christ redeemed us from the tyranny of sin and death. He showed us the depths of God's love, enabling us to share in his divine nature. The names and titles the Gospels use for him—Jesus, Christ, Son of God, and Lord—teach us about his redemptive role. This is the heart of the Paschal Mystery that we are invited into, and it is a cause for great rejoicing!

The topics covered in this part are:

Article 13 God Prepares the Way: The Roles of Mary and Joseph

Annunciation

The event in which the Archangel Gabriel came to Mary to announce that she had found favor with God and would become the mother of the Messiah.

God intends that families reflect the love and communion between the Sacred Persons of the Holy Trinity: the Father, Jesus Christ the Son, and the Holy Spirit. We have a model for this in Mary, Joseph, and Jesus, the Holy Family. Though we do not know many details of Mary and Joseph's life together, the Gospels give us glimpses of their love and devotion for each other and their faith and trust in God. It was through their family that God set in motion the events that would bring his plan for our salvation to completion. This is one of the many reasons the Church holds the family to be of central importance for our faith.

Mary's Faith and Trust

Over two thousand years ago, the angel Gabriel visited a poor, Jewish young woman. He told her that "you will conceive in your womb and bear a son, and you shall name him Jesus" (Luke 1:31). Faced with what must have been a confusing and overwhelming announcement, Mary shows

What emotions do you see in Mary's face in this beautiful icon?

© Julian Kumar/GODONG/Godong/Corbis

her complete trust and faith in God with her simple but profound answer: "I am the handmaid of the Lord. May it be done to me according to your word" (verse 38). In her unhesitating "yes" to God's invitation at the **Annunciation,** Mary committed to her role in God's plan of salvation and became *Theotokos,* meaning "God-bearer." Because of God's grace, Mary's faith was possible. By pronouncing her "fiat" at the Annunciation and giving her consent to the Incarnation, Mary was already collaborating with all that her Divine Son would bring about.

God the Father chose Mary from all the descendants of Eve to bear his Eternal Son. From the moment of her conception, Mary was free of Original Sin and she remained blameless and without personal sin for the whole of her life. This is a doctrine called the **Immaculate Conception.** Mary's cousin, Elizabeth, recognizes this truth in her greeting to Mary: "Most blessed are you among women, and blessed is the fruit of your womb" (Luke 1:42). Thus God equipped Mary to be able to give herself completely to his plan of salvation.

According to the Father's plan, Jesus Christ was born of a virgin as a sign of his divine identity. When Mary asked how she could give birth, because she was a virgin, Gabriel replied: "The holy Spirit will come upon you, and the power of the Most High will overshadow you. Therefore the child to be born will be called holy, the Son of God" (Luke 1:35). Jesus' birth is a result of divine initiative with the Virgin Mary as his mother and God the Father his only father. Joseph was not his physical father but was his earthly foster father. The virgin birth also symbolizes that Jesus is the New Adam (who also did not have an earthly father) who will usher in the new Heaven and earth that is our ultimate destiny. Mary remained a virgin her entire life, a sign of her total commitment, body and soul, to God.

Theotokos
A Greek title for Mary meaning "God bearer."

Immaculate Conception
The dogma that Mary was conceived without Original Sin and remained free from personal sin throughout her entire life.

clement
Merciful.

Pray It!

In This Valley of Tears

As you enter Saint Peter's Basilica in Vatican City, you see an extraordinary statue by Michelangelo called *La Pieta*. It depicts Mary, the Mother of God, embracing Jesus, who was just taken down from the cross. This masterpiece portrays the anguish of a mother who has lost her child. Almost any parent will tell you this is the worst pain one could ever imagine. Mary knows the depths of whatever suffering you are enduring. You can turn to her in your darkest moments. She has been there. She knows. This prayer to Mary is known as the *Salve Regina*, or Hail, Holy Queen.

Hail, holy Queen, Mother of mercy:
Hail, our life, our sweetness and our hope.
To you do we cry, poor banished children of Eve.
To you do we send up our sighs,
mourning and weeping in this valley of tears.
Turn then, most gracious advocate
your eyes of mercy towards us;
and after this our exile,
show unto us the blessed fruit of your womb, Jesus.
O **clement,** O loving, O sweet Virgin Mary.

Joseph's Faith and Trust

It is not only Mary who displays great faith and trust in God's plan. Though the Gospel of Luke emphasizes Mary's role, the Gospel of Matthew emphasizes Joseph's role. From the very beginning, we learn that Joseph is a compassionate man. Upon learning that Mary is pregnant, Matthew's Gospel tells us "Joseph her husband, since he was a righteous man, yet unwilling to expose her to shame, decided to divorce her quietly" (1:19). As a betrothed woman, Mary would have been subject to harsh penalties, even death by stoning, had Joseph chosen to accuse her of adultery.

This is where God steps in. An angel (Gabriel?) appears to Joseph in a dream and tells him the same thing the angel told Mary in the Gospel of Luke—that Mary's child was conceived through the Holy Spirit and that he was to be named Jesus. The angel tells Joseph to take the pregnant Mary into

In this African image of Jesus' birth, who might the two boys with musical instruments represent?

© Life of Jesus Mafa/www.jesusmafa.com

his home, which Joseph does without question (see Matthew 1:20–25). Later the angel appears to Joseph in another dream and warns Joseph to flee with Mary and the infant Jesus to Egypt (see 2:13–14). This is to avoid the infant massacre ordered by King Herod. After Herod dies, the angel tells Joseph it is safe to return with his family to Israel (see 2:19–21). The Gospel recounts that after both dreams Joseph rose and took the child and his mother, emphasizing his unhesitating obedience and trust in God's call. He didn't even wait until he was done sleeping!

Joseph is a model husband and father. He puts his complete trust in God, accepting both Mary's virgin pregnancy and the need to uproot his family at a moment's notice. He loves Mary wholeheartedly and does whatever he can to protect her. He cares for Jesus as his own son. He is a carpenter, most likely a stonemason, and supports his family through hard work. Because there is no mention of Joseph after the account of the lost child Jesus being found in the Temple, it is assumed that Joseph died before Jesus' public ministry. We honor Saint Joseph as the patron saint of the universal Church, of happy death, of workers, and of fathers. He is also the patron saint of many countries. His feast days are March 19 and May 1. ✝

Jesus' Brothers and Sisters

Some people ask, "How is it possible that Mary remained a virgin her whole life when the Gospels speak about Jesus' brothers and sisters?" (see Mark 3:31–35 and 6:3, for example). This is possible because of the close kinship relationships in biblical times. Extended families lived next to one another and were together every day. So a child's aunts and uncles were kind of considered to be another set of parents, and cousins were commonly called brothers and sisters. So Jesus' brothers and sisters in the Gospels were members of his extended family. They were not Mary's other children. There is also a tradition that says Joseph was a widower and had children from his first Marriage. If that were the case, Jesus could also have had stepbrothers and stepsisters.

Article 14 The Gospels and Christological Prophecies

foreshadow
To represent or prefigure a person before his or her life or an event before it occurs.

Christological
Having to do with the branch of theology called Christology. Christology is the study of the person and life of Jesus Christ, his ministry, and his mission.

How would you like to have Jesus lead you in a Bible study? Some of Jesus' disciples had that privilege soon after his Resurrection. Toward the end of the Gospel of Luke, two confused disciples were traveling home to their village after Jesus' Crucifixion (see 24:13–32). The Risen Christ appeared and walked with them, but they did not recognize him. When they told Jesus all that had happened, he "said to them, 'Oh, how foolish you are! How slow of heart to believe all that the prophets spoke! Was it not necessary that the Messiah should suffer these things and enter into his glory?' Then beginning with Moses and all the prophets, he interpreted to them what referred to him in all the scriptures" (24:25–27).

Following Jesus' example the first Christians realized how much of Jesus' life and mission was **foreshadowed** in the Old Testament Scriptures. In the article "The Growing Messianic Hope," we looked at some of these **Christological** prophecies. God was revealing how his plan would be fulfilled through his relationship with his Chosen People. The sacred authors of the New Testament frequently made reference to these Old Testament connections in order to help others believe. Those with the gift of faith recognize the truth of these prophetic passages, confirming our faith in Christ. Though not the same as a Bible study led by Jesus, the following chart provides many examples of Christological prophecies and how they were fulfilled by God's Word made flesh, Jesus Christ.

"The virgin shall be with child, and bear a son, and shall name him Immanuel." (Isaiah 7:14)

Some Christological Prophecies

There are many passages in the Old Testament that Christians have understood to be fulfilled in Jesus Christ. Here are just a few examples. Only selected parts of the passages are quoted in the chart; you may wish to look up and read the complete reference. ✞

Old Testament Prophecy	New Testament Fulfillment
The Savior will be born of a virgin.	
Isaiah 7:14: "Therefore the Lord himself will give you this sign: the virgin shall be with child, and bear a son, and shall name him Immanuel."	**Matthew 1:22–23:** "All this took place to fulfill what the Lord had said through the prophet: 'Behold, the virgin shall be with child and bear a son, and they shall name him Emmanuel,' which means 'God is with us.'"
The Savior will be born in Bethlehem.	
Micah 5:1–4a: "But you, Bethlehem-Ephrathah \ too small to be among the clans of Judah, \ From you shall come forth for me \ one who is to be ruler in Israel . . ."	**Luke 2:4–7:** "And Joseph too went up from Galilee from the town of Nazareth to Judea, to the city of David that is called Bethlehem. . . . While they were there, the time came for her to have her child, and she gave birth to her firstborn son."
The Savior will be full of zeal for God's house, the Temple.	
Psalm 69:10: "Because zeal for your house consumes me, / I am scorned by those who scorn you."	**John 2:17:** "His disciples recalled the words of scripture, 'Zeal for your house will consume me.'"
The Savior will be filled with the Spirit of God.	
Isaiah 61:1–2: "The spirit of the Lord GOD is upon me . . ."	**Luke 4:16–21:** "He [Jesus] unrolled the scroll and found the passage where it was written: 'The Spirit of the Lord is upon me.' . . . He said to them, 'Today this scripture passage is fulfilled in your hearing.'"
The Savior will come into his glory, arriving on an ass (donkey).	
Zechariah 9:9: "See, your king shall come to you; \ a just savior is he, \ Meek, and riding on an ass, \ on a colt, the foal of an ass."	**Matthew 21:4–5:** "This happened so that what had been spoken through the prophet might be fulfilled . . . 'Behold, your king comes to you, \ meek and riding on an ass, \ and on a colt, the foal of a beast of burden.'"
The Savior will be betrayed for thirty pieces of silver.	
Zechariah 11:12–13: "And they counted out my wages, thirty pieces of silver."	**Matthew 27:3–10:** "Judas, his betrayer, seeing that Jesus had been condemned, deeply regretted what he had done. He returned the thirty pieces of silver. . . ."
The Savior will suffer and die.	
Psalm 22: "My God, my God why have you abandoned me? . . . All who see me mock me. . . . As dry as a potsherd is my throat. . . . they divide my garments among them; for my clothing they cast lots." (Read the whole Psalm for many more connections to Jesus' Crucifixion.)	**Mark 15:34:** "Jesus cried out in a loud voice, *'Eloi, Eloi, lema sabachthani?'* which is translated, 'My God, my God, why have you forsaken me?'" **Mark 15:29:** "Those passing by reviled him." **John 19:28:** "Jesus said, 'I thirst.'" **John 19:23–24:** "So they said to one another, 'Let's not tear it, but cast lots for it.'" (Read the complete accounts of Jesus' Crucifixion to see other connections.)
The Savior will be the Son of God and will overcome death.	
Psalm 2:7–8: "I will proclaim the decree of the LORD, \ who said to me, "You are my son; \ today I am your father." **Psalm 16:10:** "For you will not abandon me to Sheol, \ nor let your faithful servant see the pit."	**Acts 13:32–35:** "It is written in the second psalm, 'You are my son; this day I have begotten you.'" . . . "That is why he also says in another psalm, 'You will not suffer your holy one to see corruption.'"

Article 15 Why the Word Became Flesh

All the great mysteries of our faith fit together and support one another, kind of like a three-dimensional jigsaw puzzle. This is called the **analogy of faith.** A good example of this is how the Incarnation and the Paschal Mystery are deeply connected to each other. The Paschal Mystery could not have happened without the Incarnation, and without the Paschal Mystery, there is no need for the Incarnation.

The Incarnation: A Quick Review

The mystery of the union of Jesus' divine and human natures in one Divine Person is called the **Incarnation.** Like the Trinity, the Incarnation is a mystery we will never be able to fully understand. But we do know that at the time appointed by God, Jesus Christ, the Word of God, became incarnate; that is, without losing his divine nature, he became fully man. This is expressed in the Nicene Creed when we say, "For us men and for our salvation . . . [he] was incarnate of the Virgin Mary, and became man."

Live It!

Ten Ways to Make the *Good* News *Your Good* News

1. Join or start a Bible study group.
2. Set aside a time each week to read the next Sunday's Gospel reading.
3. Keep a journal devoted to your reflections on the Sunday Gospel readings.
4. Read the Gospel of Mark from beginning to end. It will take only an hour or two!
5. Buy or check out a Bible commentary at the library to learn more about the background and history of the four Gospels.
6. Each month choose just one of Jesus' teachings and focus on incorporating it into your life.
7. Find a Bible passage you find personally meaningful and post it in your locker to inspire you.
8. Read about how saints chose to live the Good News.
9. Find a good daily reflection book that has short Bible readings for each day of the year. Start or end your day with a 3- to 5-minute reading.
10. Pray with the Sunday Gospel readings or other Bible passages (lectio divina).

The common phrase we use to describe the identity of Jesus Christ is "true God and true man." This may sound a little odd to our gender-sensitive modern ears, but we use this phrase to emphasize that the Word of God assumed human nature, and to be human always means being male or female. The phrase "true man" isn't meant to make us focus on Jesus' masculinity as much as on his humanity.

The Reasons for the Incarnation

Jesus Christ is true God and true man, in the unity of his divine Person. Because of this, he is the one and only mediator between God and humanity. Here are some of the spiritual results of the Incarnation, and the reasons why it was needed.

To Reconcile Us with God through the Forgiveness of Sins

After the Fall human beings were separated from full communion with God because of our sins. But through the Incarnation, Christ took upon himself all human sin so that we might be reconciled with God. As Saint Paul explains it, "For just as through the disobedience of one person the many were made sinners, so through the obedience of one the many will be made righteous" (Romans 5:19). Or put another way by the author of the First Letter of John, "In this is love: not that we have loved God, but that he loved us and sent his Son as **expiation** for our sins" (4:10).

That We Might Know the Depth of God's Love

After the Fall and the resulting shame that accompanies sin (remember Adam and Eve hiding from God?), humanity did not experience or understand the true nature of God's unconditional love for us. Thus the first Christians were astounded at the realization that God loved us so much he would take on human nature and even suffer a torturous death to redeem us. This is referred to again and again in the New Testament writings. "For God so loved the world that he gave his only Son, so that everyone who believes in him might not perish but might have eternal life" (John 3:16). "Indeed, only with difficulty does one die for a just person, though perhaps for a good person one might even find cour-

analogy of faith
The coherence of individual doctrines with the whole of Revelation. In other words, as each doctrine is connected with Revelation, each doctrine is also connected with all other doctrines.

Incarnation
From the Latin, meaning "to become flesh," referring to the biblical Revelation that Jesus is both true God and true man.

expiation
The act of atoning for sin or wrongdoing.

age to die. But God proves his love for us in that while we were still sinners Christ died for us" (Romans 5:7–8).

To Be Our Model of Holiness

As God, Jesus Christ is perfect holiness. As a man, he shows us how to be holy in our everyday lives. We are given frequent commands in the Gospel to imitate Christ's holiness. At the Transfiguration, God the Father commands: "This is my beloved Son. Listen to him" (Mark 9:7). In the Gospel of John, at the Last Supper, Jesus tells his disciples (and us), "This is my commandment: love one another as I love you" (15:12).

Moses and Elijah appear with Jesus in the Transfiguration. Moses represents that Jesus is the fulfillment of the Law of God and Elijah represents that Jesus fulfills the mission of the prophets.

© Life of Jesus Mafa/www.jesusmafa.com

Catholic Wisdom

We Are Christ's Body

After the resurrected Christ ascended into Heaven, is he still present among us in a physical way? In this inspiring quotation, Saint Teresa of Ávila reminds us that if we follow Jesus as our model of holiness, he is present among us in a very real way:

Christ has no body now but yours;
No hands, no feet on earth but yours;
Yours are the eyes through which He looks compassion on this world;
Yours are the feet with which He is to go about doing good.
Yours are the hands with which He is to bless us now.

To Make Us Partakers of the Divine Nature

Christ wants us to share in his divinity! This amazing truth means God wants us to share in his divine life and to become the image of God we were created to be. Saint Athanasius, a Church Father who lived in the fourth century, explained it like this:

> He [the Son of God] became man so that we might be made God; and he manifested himself in the flesh, so that we might grasp the idea of the unseen Father; and he endured the insolence of men, so that we might receive the inheritance of immortality.

> (Treatise on the Incarnation of the Word)

Saint Athanasius

Saint Athanasius was born near Alexandria about the year AD 295. He became bishop of Alexandria in AD 328. He did not have a peaceful time as bishop. Athanasius had to defend the Church against Arianism, a heresy that taught that Jesus was not fully God; he was only partially divine, sort of halfway between God and man. The proponents of Arianism were very strong, and five times they forced Athanasius to leave Alexandria and go into exile. But in the end, Athanasius's defense of the true faith was victorious and he was able to spend the last years of his life in peace. He died in AD 373 and was declared a Doctor of the Church.

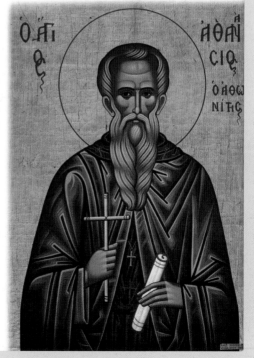

To Destroy the Power of the Devil

A previous article discussed the spiritual war between the Devil and the forces of evil and God and the forces of good. On our own, humanity could not hope to defeat Satan. But Jesus resists the temptations of Satan in the desert, anticipating his complete victory over evil with his Passion, death, and Resurrection. "Indeed, the Son of God was revealed to destroy the works of the devil" (1 John 3:8). We share in Jesus' victory over Satan. Strengthened by our faith and the gifts of the Spirit, Satan has lost his power over us. ✝

Article 16 The Titles Say It All

We commonly give titles to people to recognize their role and their importance in society. Calling someone Father, Doctor, Captain, Professor, President, or Bishop immediately tells us important information about that person. The same is true for Jesus. In the New Testament, Jesus is given a variety of titles that indicate his central role in salvation history. We conclude this section by reflecting on the meaning of the name of Jesus and three of his most important titles. Think about these titles for Jesus as you use them in your prayer, reverently remembering the tremendous love of God each of them represents.

© Hazlan Abdul Hakim/iStockphoto

Christ Jesus

Lord Son of God

Jesus

In the beginning of the Gospel of Luke, the angel Gabriel instructs Mary, "You will conceive in your womb and bear a son, and you shall name him Jesus" (1:31). *Jesus* means "God saves" in Hebrew (Joshua is another form of Jesus' name). Jesus' very name reflects his divine identity and his mission as Savior of the world. It is through the Paschal Mystery that we are saved from our sins, which is why the Father "bestowed on him the name \ that is above every name, \ that at the name of Jesus \ every knee should bend, \ of those in heaven and on earth and under the earth" (Philippians 2:9–10).

Christ

Christ is not Jesus' last name, even though it sounds like we use it that way. It is a formal title for Jesus that is used more than four hundred times in the New Testament. *Christ* is the Greek translation of the Hebrew word *messiah,* which means "anointed." To be anointed in the religious sense is to have oil placed on you in preparation for a special mission. In the Old Testament, kings, priests, and prophets were anointed in God's name. Jesus is Christ because the Father anointed him with the Holy Spirit and established him as priest, prophet, and king.

After their kingdom collapsed, many Jews believed God would send a new anointed one, the Messiah (or Christ), who would fulfill all God's promises for salvation. Peter was the first to proclaim about Jesus, "You are the Messiah" (Mark 8:29), announcing that Jesus was the savior the Jews had been hoping for. So when you say "Jesus Christ," you are really saying "Jesus, the Anointed One sent by God to be the Savior of the world."

Son of God

Another title frequently used for Jesus is Son of God. In the Old Testament, the title "son of God" is sometimes used for angels, for the people of Israel, and for Israel's kings. The title signifies their special relationship with God. But when it is applied to Jesus in the New Testament, it takes on additional meaning. We are all children of God, but Jesus has a unique relationship with the Father. At both Jesus' Baptism and his

Transfiguration, the Father's voice announces, "This is my beloved Son" (Matthew 3:17, 17:5). Jesus is the only begotten Son of the Father, and he is the Second Person of the Trinity, fully God himself. It is because Jesus is both true God and true man, that he is the one and only mediator who can restore the damaged relationship between God and humanity.

Lord

Jesus is frequently referred to as Lord in the New Testament. Lord was a title of respect in Jesus' time, and frequently people who were approaching Jesus respectfully called him Lord. But the word had another unique meaning. *Lord* is the Greek word the Jews used for God instead of calling him *Yahweh,* the Hebrew name often used for God in the Old Testament. *Yahweh* was considered too sacred to be pro-

Other New Testament Titles for Jesus Christ

Besides the three primary titles explained in this article, many other titles for Jesus are mentioned in the New Testament. Here are some of them.

Title	Location
Alpha and Omega	Revelation 22:13
Bread of Life	John 6:48
Bright Morning Star	Revelation 22:16
God Our Savior	Titus 3:4
Good Shepherd	John 10:11
High Priest	Hebrews 3:1
King of Kings	Revelation 19:16
Lamb of God	John 1:29
Light of the World	John 8:12
Lord of Lords	Revelation 19:16
Paschal Lamb	1 Corinthians 5:7
the Resurrection and the Life	John 11:25
the Way, the Truth, and the Life	John 14:6
the Word	John 1:1

nounced out loud in public. When Thomas calls Jesus "My Lord and my God!" (John 20:28), he is calling Jesus by a title the Jews used for God. Today, whenever we call Jesus Lord, we too recognize his divinity and acknowledge that he alone is worthy of our worship and our complete obedience. ♱

Part Review

1. Why was it important that Mary conceived and gave birth as a virgin?

2. How did Joseph show his trust in God and his love for Mary and Jesus?

3. Give some examples of the Christological prophecies.

4. Why is Jesus the perfect and only mediator between God and humanity?

5. Give three reasons for the Incarnation.

6. What is the meaning of the name Jesus?

7. What does the title Christ reveal about Jesus?

Part 2

The Redemptive Nature of Christ's Earthly Life

The Father's saving plan is revealed through his Son, Jesus Christ, and fully understood with the guidance of the Holy Spirit. All of Jesus' life teaches us about God's saving plan: his poverty, his humility, his prayer, whom he lived with, whom he called to be his disciples, his teaching and preaching, his healings, his exorcisms . . . everything.

Christ's Passion, death, Resurrection, and Ascension most clearly reveal his and his Father's glory (see John 13:31). These events, which we identify with the Paschal Mystery, the fulfillment of God's plan of salvation, are the focus of the next section. In this part we focus on how the mystery of redemption is already at work in the words and actions of Jesus that precede his Passion.

The topics covered in this part are:

Article 17 The Luminous Mysteries

In 2002 Pope John Paul II issued the apostolic letter "*Rosarium Virginis Mariae*" ("The Rosary of the Virgin Mary"). In the letter he recommends a change in the way the Rosary is prayed. In addition to the three traditional sets of mysteries that are meditated on when praying the Rosary—the joyful mysteries, the sorrowful mysteries, and the glorious mysteries—the Pope recommends another set of mysteries, which he calls the luminous mysteries or the mysteries of light. These five mysteries are significant moments in Jesus' public ministry where he is most clearly identified as the Messiah, the Savior, the Son of God. In these events he is "the light of the world" (John 9:5) shining for all to see!

The Luminous Mysteries

The five luminous mysteries of the Rosary highlight events in Jesus' public ministry where he is most clearly revealed as the light of the world.

Mystery	Scripture Passage	Description
The Baptism in the Jordan	Matthew 3:13–17, Mark 1:9–11, Luke 3:21–22, John 1:31–34	The voice of the Father declares Jesus the beloved Son.
The Wedding at Cana	John 2:1–12	Christ changes water into wine, his first public miracle.
The Proclamation of the Kingdom	Mark 2:15 is a good summary.	Jesus calls to conversion (see Mark 1:15) and forgives the sins of all who draw near to him.
The Transfiguration	Matthew 17:1–8, Mark 9:2–8, Luke 9:28–36	The glory of the Godhead shines forth from the face of Christ.
The Institution of the Eucharist	Matthew 26:26–30, Mark 14:22–26, Luke 22:14–23, 1 Corinthians 11:23–25	Jesus offers his Body and Blood as food under the signs of bread and wine.

In his letter Pope John Paul says, "Each of these mysteries is *a revelation of the Kingdom now present in the very person of Jesus*" (21). Think of the Kingdom of God as that "place" (it really is not a place in the geographic sense) where the fullness of God's grace is present and human beings are restored to full communion with God and with one another. The full realization of the **Kingdom of God** is the end result of God's saving plan. What the Pope is saying is that Jesus does not just talk about God's saving plan, he makes it real. When Jesus speaks and acts, the Kingdom of God is present to those who listen to him and believe in him. So let us consider what the five mysteries of light reveal about the Kingdom of God and the Paschal Mystery.

The Baptism in the Jordan

The account of Jesus' Baptism is told in all four Gospels, which in itself is a sign of its importance. Jesus is baptized by his cousin John. John prepares the way for Jesus, and his ministry is seen as a fulfillment of a prophecy by Isaiah (see Mark 1:2–3). John does this by urging people to reform their lives and turn away from sin. As a sign of their cleansing and renewal, he baptized people in the waters of the Jordan River.

The Baptism of Jesus is the first Luminous Mystery. Since Jesus is without sin, why did he choose to be baptized?

© Brooklyn Museum/Corbis

Even though Jesus was free from all sin, he came to John to be baptized at the beginning of his public ministry. In doing this he showed his willingness to completely identify with the human condition. By identifying himself with human sin, Jesus Christ became the perfect offering to save us from our sin. Saint Paul put it this way: "For our sake he [the Father] made him [the Son] to be sin who did not know sin, so that we might become the righteousness of God in him" (2 Corinthians 5:21).

Jesus' Baptism is an example of his perfect obedience to his heavenly Father (see "The Obedience of Christ" article). His Baptism also reveals the mystery of the Holy Trinity. The three Divine Persons of the

Trinity work together in the plan of salvation. The Holy Spirit descends upon the Son in the form of a dove and the Father pronounces, "You are my beloved Son; with you I am well pleased" (Mark 1:11). As Jesus' public ministry begins, the first Luminous Mystery shows that Jesus is the Second Person of the Trinity and he has come to save us from our sins.

The Wedding at Cana

The second Luminous Mystery is recorded in the Gospel of John only. It is a few days after Jesus' Baptism, and Jesus is attending a wedding feast with his new disciples. When the wedding party runs out of wine (which would have been an embarrassing situation for the hosts), Jesus' mother asks him to help. You probably know Jesus' response; he turns the water in six large ceremonial jars into excellent wine. The Gospel of John tells us that "Jesus did this as the beginning of his signs in Cana in Galilee and so revealed his glory, and his disciples began to believe in him" (2:11).

John's Gospel contains only seven miracles. Each of these is a sign that reveals Jesus as the Son of God. This first sign shows his power over creation. His mother already believed in him, because she asked him to do something miraculous. But now his disciples begin to believe too. The second Luminous Mystery recalls the time in which Christ began his public ministry.

The Proclamation of the Kingdom

The third Luminous Mystery is not just one event or one teaching. Through many miracles and many teachings, Jesus proclaims that the Kingdom of God is at hand. His very first words in the Gospel of Mark are these: "This is the time of fulfillment. The kingdom of God is at hand. Repent, and believe in the gospel" (1:15). The prophets had prophesied about the coming of the Kingdom of God (see Isaiah 2:2–4, Micah 4:1–4) when original justice and holiness would be restored and people would live in peace with God and one another. They prophesied that a messiah would usher in this kingdom by bringing good news to the poor and freedom to captives (see Isaiah 61:1–2).

Kingdom of God
The culmination or goal of God's plan of salvation, the Kingdom of God is announced by the Gospel and present in Jesus Christ. The Kingdom is the reign or rule of God over the hearts of people and, as a consequence of that, the development of a new social order based on unconditional love. The fullness of God's Kingdom will not be realized until the end of time. Also called the Reign of God or the Kingdom of Heaven.

Passover

The night the Lord passed over the houses of the Israelites marked by the blood of the lamb, and spared the firstborn sons from death. It also is the feast that celebrates the deliverance of the Chosen People from bondage in Egypt and the Exodus from Egypt to the Promised Land.

Eucharist, the

Also called the Mass or Lord's Supper, and based on a word for "thanksgiving," it is the central Christian liturgical celebration, established by Jesus at the Last Supper. In the Eucharist the sacrificial death and Resurrection of Jesus are both remembered and renewed. The term sometimes refers specifically to the consecrated bread and wine that have become the Body and Blood of Christ.

institute

To introduce, establish, or inaugurate.

Jesus fulfilled these ancient prophecies. His words were good news for the poor and challenging news for the wealthy (see "The Poverty of Christ" article). He lived a life of unconditional love and forgiveness, even forgiving his torturers and killers. He called everyone to forsake hate, revenge, violence, and greed. He helped the blind to see and the lame to walk. He brought freedom to those held captive by demons, disease, sin, and even death. Wherever he went, the Kingdom of God was present for those who put their faith in him. The third Luminous Mystery reveals that the Kingdom of God is present in Jesus Christ, and his life brings salvation to our world.

The Transfiguration

The fourth Luminous Mystery is captured in all three of the synoptic Gospels. The event happens soon after Peter proclaims that Jesus is the Messiah, the Son of God (see Matthew 16:16). Jesus responds to this act of faith by predicting his Passion, death, and Resurrection (see verse 21). It would seem that Jesus wanted to be clear that as Messiah he would not be a warrior leader but a suffering servant. This was hard for the disciples to hear (see verse 22).

It was just a few days later that Jesus took Peter, James, and John to the top of a mountain by themselves. There Jesus was transfigured and the three disciples saw him in his glory; Christ's face and clothes shone like the sun and both Moses and Elijah appeared with Christ (see Matthew 17:1–3). To top things off, the Father's voice came from the clouds saying, "This is my beloved Son, with whom I am well pleased; listen to him" (verse 5).

To faithful Jews, Moses represented the Law and Elijah represented the message of all the prophets. Their appearance with Jesus was a sign that Jesus was the fulfillment of the Law and the prophets. The Transfiguration reassured Peter, James, and John that Jesus was indeed the Messiah. It strengthened their faith before the ordeal of Jesus' Passion and death. The fourth Luminous Mystery reveals that Jesus was the one they had been waiting for, but they would not fully understand the plan of salvation until the principal events of the Paschal Mystery—Christ's Passion, death, Resurrection, and Ascension—had come to their conclusion.

The Institution of the Eucharist

The fifth Luminous Mystery is testified to in the synoptic Gospels and in Paul's First Letter to the Corinthians and is strongly implied in the Gospel of John. These all testify that soon before his death, at a **Passover** meal, Jesus turned ordinary bread and wine into his sacred Body and Blood and shared these with the Twelve Apostles. Then he commanded them to "do this in memory of me" (Luke 22:19). This was the first celebration of the **Eucharist,** which today we also call the Mass. By **instituting** the Eucharist, Jesus gave the Church a great gift—the gift of himself—present to us in his Body and Blood.

This Luminous Mystery, the institution of the Eucharist, reveals that Jesus Christ is the Lamb of God, whose life is given that we might be freed from sin and death. Just as the original Paschal Lamb was offered to free the people of Israel from their slavery in Egypt, so through his Passion, death, Resurrection, and Ascension, Jesus' life is offered up for us. This is the core of the Paschal Mystery, which we enter into every time we participate in the Eucharist. This is why "the Eucharist is the heart and summit of the Church's life, for in it Christ associates his Church and all her members with his sacrifice of praise and thanksgiving offered once for all on the cross to his Father; by this sacrifice he pours out the graces of salvation on his Body which is the Church" (*Catechism of the Catholic Church [CCC]*, 1407). ✝

Notice how the color of Jesus' tunic stands out in this image of the Last Supper. What symbolic meaning might his red garment have?

© Life of Jesus Mafa/www.jesusmafa.com

Article 18 The Poverty of Christ

redeem, Redeemer, redemption

From the Latin *redemptio*, meaning "a buying back"; to redeem something is to pay the price for its freedom. In the Old Testament, it refers to Yahweh's deliverance of Israel and, in the New Testament, to Christ's deliverance of all Christians from the forces of sin. Christ our Redeemer paid the price to free us from the slavery of sin and bring about our redemption.

In the musical *Jesus Christ Superstar*, Judas rhetorically asks Jesus why he chose to reveal himself the way he did. Why be born and live in an unimportant place? Why be born in a poor and unimportant family? Wouldn't Jesus' message be more easily accepted if he were born into an important family? Wouldn't it be more easily heard if he went to Rome and preached and lived in the center of the world's politics and economics?

These are important questions because everything in Jesus' life does indeed teach us about God's plan for our **redemption.** Let us start with Jesus' humble beginnings. There is a reason he was born into poverty and lived in relative poverty—it has something to teach us and will lead us more deeply into the Paschal Mystery.

Elites and Non-Elites

In the United States, we are used to a socioeconomic system where there is a minority of wealthy people, a minority of poor people, and a majority of middle-class people. In Jesus' time there were basically two economic classes: the elites (the wealthy) and the non-elites (the poor). The elites were a very small minority of the population, but they owned most of the land, lived in luxury and plenty, and held all the political and economic power. They lived almost exclusively in cities and rented out their land to tenant farmers who paid big rents and taxes to the elites.

Olives were a cash crop grown by wealthy landowners in Jesus' time.

© Saint Mary's Press/Brian Singer-Towns

The non-elites were the vast majority of the people. They were lucky to make just enough to survive. If they owned a small plot of land, they were constantly in danger of hunger or starvation if their crops failed. Many worked as day laborers for the wealthy landowners who grew **cash crops,** not **subsistence crops.** Some non-elites were "self-employed," but they had to pay high fees (to fish, for example) or rents (to use someone's fishing boat, for example). They all had to pay high taxes to support both the elite Jewish leaders and the elite of the Roman Empire. Many non-elites sold themselves into slavery to work for the elites because they were at least usually assured of food and a place to sleep.

This was Jesus' world. The Gospel of Luke emphasizes Jesus' poverty. First, it shows Mary and Joseph under the power of the elites of the Roman Empire. At the order of the Emperor, Caesar Augustus, they have to make the difficult trip from Nazareth to Bethlehem even though it is late in Mary's pregnancy (see 2:1–5). The only reason for this trip is for a census, to determine the amount of taxes the Romans would collect. The birth of Jesus in Bethlehem emphasizes Mary and Joseph's low status: "She wrapped him [Jesus] in swaddling clothes and laid him in a manger, because there was no room for them in the inn" (verse 7).

You might think that in his life Jesus would show us how to get ahead by working hard to become an elite. Instead he does just the opposite; he embraces the poverty he is born into. He resists Satan's temptation to become an elite and replies to Satan, "One does not live by bread alone" (Luke 4:4). When a scribe wishes to follow him, Jesus warns the scribe about the poverty involved in following Jesus: "Foxes have dens and birds of the sky have nests, but the Son of Man has nowhere to rest his head" (Matthew 8:20). In the parable about the Final Judgment, Jesus identifies with the poor, saying, "Whatever you did for one of these least brothers of mine, you did for me" (25:40).

cash crops
Crops that are grown to make the most wealth for the landowner but typically do not provide the basic food needed for the majority of people. In ancient Israel examples of these crops would be grapes, olives, and wheat.

subsistence crops
Crops that provide the basic food to feed the most people. In ancient Israel examples of these crops would be barley, beans, and figs.

Catholic Wisdom

Mother Teresa on Wealth

Blessed Mother Teresa of Calcutta worked with the poorest of the poor in India for over fifty years. She once said:

> I think it must be harder to be happy if you are wealthy because you may find it difficult to see God: you'll have too many other things to think about. However, if God has given you this gift of wealth, then use it for his purpose—help others, help the poor, create jobs, give work to others. Don't waste your wealth.

Material Poverty and Poverty of Heart

poverty of heart

The recognition of our deep need for God and the commitment to put God above everything else in life, particularly above the accumulation of material wealth.

Jesus embraced material poverty for one simple reason; he was teaching that we do not achieve salvation through material wealth. This was a popular belief at the time. Many Jews believed that material wealth was a sign that you were blessed by God and living a righteous life. Jesus taught just the opposite: "Blessed are you who are poor, / for the kingdom of God is yours. . . . But woe to you who are rich, / for you have received your consolation" (Luke 6:20,24).

Not only did Jesus teach that God had not abandoned the poor, but he also taught that the elites, the wealthy, have a special obligation to help the poor. There are several Gospel stories about this:

- the parable of the rich young man (see Matthew 19:16–24)
- the parable of the rich man and Lazarus (see Luke 16:19–31)
- the parable of the Final Judgment (see Matthew 25:31–46)
- the parable of whom to invite to eat with you (see Luke 14:12–14)
- the parable of the wedding banquet (see Luke 14:15–24)

Consider the two homes in this image. Do people seem happier in the large, wealthier home or in the smaller home?

Jesus' life and teaching revealed that **poverty of heart** (sometimes called spiritual poverty) is necessary for us to be

© James B. Janknegt

truly in communion with God. Those people with poverty of heart recognize their need for God. This is why Jesus says, "Blessed are the poor in spirit" (Matthew 5:3). Without God we are truly empty and alone; no amount of material wealth can fill that void. In fact, material wealth often gets in the way of our recognizing our need for God. For this reason Jesus warns us that material wealth can be dangerous to our salvation: "How hard it is for those who have wealth to enter the kingdom of God!" (Mark 10:23). He calls us to be unattached to material wealth. Material wealth is not bad in and of itself, but it is very easy to let it take the place of God in our lives.

Money can be a very touchy subject. Our culture places a great deal of importance on having it. We often measure our worth by how much we have. We get stressed when we don't think we have enough—which for many people is most of the time. We sometimes compromise our values and even our physical and emotional well-being in order to get more. The poverty of Jesus challenges us to put our trust in God, not in money. When we do this, we are one step closer to the Kingdom of God. ✝

Gospel Teaching on Poverty of Heart

There are many places in the four Gospels in which Jesus teaches about the importance of poverty of heart.

Gospel Passage	Summary
Matthew 6:19–21,24	"store up treasures in heaven" and "no one can serve two masters"
Matthew 13:44–46	treasure buried in the field, the pearl of great price
Mark 12:41–44	widow's mite
Luke 12:15–21	parable of the rich fool
Luke 12:22–32	do not worry about what to eat or what to wear
Luke 12:33–34	"where your treasure is, there also will your heart be"

Article 19 The Obedience of Christ

Obedience is a topic that can irritate many people. We sometimes rebel or complain when we are told what to do by people in positions of authority. Part of our resistance to the idea of obedience is probably rooted in our historical struggle against unjust situations. For example, the United States was born when our ancestors rejected the English monarchy and disobeyed unfair laws. So why then is obedience such an important value to our faith?

The answer lies in whom you are obedient to. We owe our obedience to God, our Creator, who calls us back to full, loving communion with him. To redeem Adam's disobedience and to be an example for us, the Son of God lived a life of perfect obedience to his Father.

Redeeming Adam's Disobedience

Our first parents disobeyed God, and through their disobedience brought sin and death into the world. To rescue us from this situation, the Son of God assumed a human nature, becoming our perfect mediator. Through Christ's perfect obedience to his Father's will, he restores human nature to its original holiness. Says Saint Paul, "For just as through the disobedience of one person the many were made sinners, so through the obedience of one the many will be made righteous" (Romans 5:19). This is why we call Jesus the New Adam.

Jesus' greatest act of obedience for the first Christians was his willingness to assume a human nature. They even had a hymn about this that Paul quotes in Philippians 2:5–8:

> Have among yourselves the same attitude that is also yours in Christ Jesus,
>
> Who, though he was in the form of God,
>   did not regard equality with God
>   something to be grasped.
>   Rather, he emptied himself,
>   taking the form of a slave,
>   coming in human likeness;
>   and found human in appearance,
>   he humbled himself,
>   becoming obedient to death,
>   even death on a cross.

This painting portrays Jesus' suffering in the garden at Gethsemane. What are the angels showing Jesus that causes him such agony? When does obedience require you to make a personal sacrifice?

© Brooklyn Museum/Corbis

Jesus' Example of Obedience

Paul introduces the Philippians' hymn with these directions: "Have among yourselves the same attitude that is also yours in Christ Jesus." Jesus' obedience to his Father's will is the model for us of how to live a life of obedience to God. First, Jesus was obedient in his human relationships, respecting the order his Father created. We read how as a child he respected his earthly parents: "He went down with them and came to Nazareth, and was obedient to them" (Luke 2:51). Tradition teaches us that in the hidden years of Jesus' life, which are not recorded in the Gospels, he remained obedient to Mary and Joseph.

Second, Jesus was obedient to his heavenly Father. In the garden at Gethsemane, we see his obedience even when it would lead to torture and death. Knowing that his Passion and death are coming, Jesus prays that he might escape this ordeal. But he concludes his prayer with a commitment to obediently follow his Father's will: "If it is not possible that this cup pass without my drinking it, your will be done!" (Matthew 26:42). We should never assume that obedience always came easily to Jesus and that he never struggled with it.

We are called to follow Jesus' example to be obedient to his Father's will, not because God wants to control us as a puppeteer controls puppets but because God is a perfectly loving parent who wants what is best for us. When we are obedient to him, we grow in holiness, which is to say we grow to be in closer communion with him. The First Letter of Peter gives excellent advice:

> Like obedient children, do not act in compliance with the desires of your former ignorance but, as he who called you is holy, be holy yourselves in every aspect of your conduct, for it is written, "Be holy because I [am] holy." (1:14–16) ☨

Christ Our Teacher

Saint Clement of Alexandria (AD 150–211) traveled from Greece, to Italy, to Palestine, and finally to Egypt to find Christian teachers to instruct him in the faith. Here is an excerpt on his thought about Christ as our Teacher:

> The Word by whom all things were made, has appeared as our Teacher; and he, who bestowed life upon us in the beginning, when, as our Creator, he formed us, now that he has appeared as our Teacher, has taught us to live well so that, afterwards, as God, he might furnish us abundantly with eternal life.
>
> (Exhortation to the Greeks)

© Foto Marburg/Art Resource, NY

Article 20 Christ's Moral Preaching

Christ's moral teaching is perhaps the section of the Gospels that Christians struggle with most. For in his moral teaching, he goes beyond the letter of the Old Law to challenge us to live the deeper moral truths the Old Law is intended to teach us, thus revealing its ultimate meaning. In his life and teaching, he perfectly fulfills the Old Law and ushers in the New Law. Even more, through the Paschal Mystery, he redeems us from all our sins against the Law. Living the New Law is a return to original holiness and justice. It can only be lived with the sanctifying grace given by the Holy Spirit through Baptism.

The New Law is part of the Paschal Mystery; through the New Law, Christ redeems us by purifying our **conscience.** When we live according to the New Law, our moral choices are not based on only what is good or bad for us, or based on **legalistic** morality, but are based on what truly brings us into full communion with God and with one another. Jesus sums up the New Law in two great commandments: "The first is this: 'Hear, O Israel! The Lord our God is Lord alone! You shall love the Lord your God with all your heart, with all your soul, with all your mind, and with all your strength.' The second is this: 'You shall love your neighbor as yourself'" (Mark 12:29–31). In this article we take a closer look at Jesus' expression of the New Law in the Sermon on the Mount.

conscience

The "interior voice" of a person, a God-given sense of the law of God. Moral conscience leads people to understand themselves as responsible for their actions, and prompts them to do good and avoid evil. To make good judgments, one needs to have a well-formed conscience.

legalistic

To focus strictly on what the law requires without considering the truth the law is intended to promote. Jesus taught that all law must be an expression of love for God and love for our neighbor.

© Life of Jesus Mafa/www.jesusmafa.com

Jesus teaches his followers how to live as true children of God. What part of Jesus' moral teaching is most challenging for you?

The Sermon on the Mount

The Sermon on the Mount is found in Matthew, chapters 5–7. Some have called the Sermon on the Mount a kind of "mini-Gospel" because it is a summary of the key teachings of Jesus. We are going to focus on three of the "You have heard it said" statements in chapter five of the sermon. These statements are good examples of how Jesus purifies our conscience by teaching us the true meaning of God's Law. If you haven't read the Sermon on the Mount recently, it would be good to do so before reading the rest of this article.

"You have heard that it was said to your ancestors, 'You shall not kill; and whoever kills will be liable to judgment.' But I say to you, whoever is angry with his brother will be liable to judgment" (Matthew 5:21–22).

The Old Law commands us not to kill. This may seem obvious, but recall the story of Cain and Abel. The first sin after the Fall was murder. What the Old Law is meant to teach us is that thoughts and attitudes—anger, hatred, lack of forgiveness, revenge—that lead to violence are wrong in themselves. They have no place in the Kingdom of God. They will not lead to love and communion with other people and with God.

Outline of the Sermon on the Mount (Matthew, Chapters 5–7)

5:3–12	the Beatitudes
5:13–16	salt of the earth, light of the world
5:17–20	teaching about the Law
5:21–33	teachings about anger, adultery, divorce, and oaths
5:38–48	teachings about retaliation and love of enemies
6:1–18	teachings about almsgiving, prayer, and fasting
6:19–34	teachings about poverty of heart
7:1–12	teachings about judging others, relying on God, the Golden Rule
7:13–23	teachings on discipleship
7:24–29	the result of acting on Jesus' teachings

Does this mean that every time you have an angry thought you are sinning? No, those thoughts are part of life, especially as we are on the journey to perfect holiness. What is sinful is to hang on to feelings of anger and hurt; letting them grow inside us until they become thoughts of revenge. At that point we are only one step away from actually hurting the other person. The New Law calls us to let go of our anger and replace it with forgiveness and compassion, even for those who hurt us.

chastity
The virtue by which people are able to successfully and healthfully integrate their sexuality into their total person; recognized as one of the fruits of the Holy Spirit. Also one of the vows of religious life.

"You have heard that it was said, 'You shall not commit adultery.' But I say to you, everyone who looks at a woman with lust has already committed adultery with her in his heart" (Matthew 5:27–28).

The Old Law commands us not to have sex outside of Marriage. Again Jesus says this is just a minimum requirement. The Old Law is meant to teach us that the thoughts and attitudes that lead to sexual promiscuity are wrong in themselves. Christ's New Law commands us to live lives of **chastity** and not to think or act in ways that might lead us to sexual sin.

This is a difficult commandment to live out in our culture. Sexuality and sexual suggestion are often used as marketing techniques, and we are constantly bombarded with sexual messages. This makes it difficult to go through a day without having a sexual thought! Again this doesn't mean that having a brief sexual thought is sinful. What is sinful is to hang on to those thoughts, letting them grow into sexual fantasies and then convincing yourself that acting on those thoughts and fantasies is okay. The New Law asks us to let go of sexual fantasies and avoid sexual temptations and live chaste lives.

"You have heard that it was said, 'You shall love your neighbor and hate your enemy.' But I say to you, love your enemies, and pray for those who persecute you" (5:43–44).

Jesus quotes Leviticus 19:18, which says that you should love your neighbor as yourself (it does not say anything about hating enemies). In Jesus' time people were fiercely loyal to their own family and social groups, distrusting everyone who was outside those groups. By his example Jesus shows them a different way of living. He gathers people together who aren't blood relatives or even from the same social groups. He brings together fisherman, tax collectors, and zealots; these people usually distrust one another, but Jesus teaches them how to love one another.

This doesn't seem to be much different today. People often fear and distrust people who come from somewhere else. Sometimes cultural differences lead to hatred and attacks on people and their way of life. Jesus tells us these attitudes are wrong and sinful. His New Law asks us to love everyone, even

Why is caring for the earth an important moral issue?

© Tim Pannell/Corbis

Live It!

Loving Beyond Boundaries

Jesus gathered people from many different walks of life who probably, in most circumstances, hated one another. Similarly, in many schools today, certain social groups dislike and avoid one another because of their race, religion, economic status, or even something as trivial as involvement in particular extracurricular activities. Jesus saw beyond the external ways people define one another. He saw the common humanity of the fisherman and the tax collector, the Jew and the Gentile, the prostitute and the Pharisee, the zealot and the Roman soldier. And he loved them all.

Christ also asks us to look beyond the things that divide us. Though it is easy to love people we like, God requires more from us. Christians are called to love and respect athletes, band members, cheerleaders, slackers, straight-A students, and artists—everyone—whether we like them or not.

those who aren't like us and those who attack us. Through prayer, and with the help of God, we will find ways to overcome misunderstanding, distrust, and even hatred.

Jesus' moral teaching shows us what our relationship with God and others must be to participate in the Kingdom of God. Through Baptism we receive the grace that is necessary to live according to the New Law. Through the other Sacraments, we receive additional graces that strengthen us as we journey to perfection in our lives as true children of God, members of the Body of Christ, and citizens of the Kingdom of Heaven. ✝

Article 21 Christ's Healings

Being sick is no fun. Illness makes our daily routine even more challenging, if not impossible. It often isolates us from other people. People with lifelong disabilities must face these things every day. And serious illness and disease force us to face death itself, which can be frightening for many people. But remember, this is not the way God intended us to be; this is the result of Original Sin.

In his public ministry, Jesus performs many miraculous healings. He cures the blind, the deaf, and the lame. He brings health and wholeness to lepers so they can rejoin the community. He casts out evil spirits from those who are possessed. Jesus has great compassion for those who are suffering and outcast. But he doesn't try to heal everyone, even though there is great need. Have you ever wondered why Jesus did not make healing his full-time ministry? The answer is that Jesus' mission was bigger than just being a miracle worker.

Jesus' healings are a sign that the Father's plan of salvation is being fulfilled. Every healing is a sign that Christ is restoring the wholeness of body, mind, and spirit he intended people to have. The healings are also signs that Jesus is the Messiah who is making the Kingdom of God present to all those who believe in him. Jesus himself points to this. When asked, "Are you the one to come, or should we look for another?" he replies, "Go and tell John what you hear and see: the blind regain their sight, the lame walk, lepers are cleansed, the deaf hear, the dead are raised, and

exorcism
The act of freeing someone from demonic possession. Exorcisms are also part of the Church's worship and prayer life, calling on the name of Christ to protect us from the power of Satan.

the poor have the good news proclaimed to them" (Matthew 11:3–5). Finally, Jesus' healings are a promise that in the Kingdom of Heaven we will all be made whole, physically and spiritually, and there will be no more suffering or sickness or disease for all God's holy ones.

Sickness and Health in Biblical Cultures

The culture Jesus lived in did not make the distinction that we do between the natural world and the spiritual world. Illness and disability were most often associated with impurity and sin. When someone is sick today, we look for a natural cause. When someone was ill at the time of Jesus, people looked for a supernatural or spiritual cause. In the Book of Job, Job's friends were convinced that his sufferings were sent by God as punishment for sins. In the Gospel of John, Jesus is asked, "Rabbi, who sinned, this man or his parents, that he was born blind?" (9:2). Jesus denies that suffering is a direct punishment for sin (see 9:3, Luke 13:1–5). But he does

Pray It!

Comfort for the Sick

Being sick is awful. We stay at home to keep others from getting sick. We are cut off from our friends. We fall behind in our schoolwork. We then get worried and upset about everything we have to do after we get better. It can be depressing! It is obvious that our physical health has an impact on our mental and spiritual health. When the Sacrament of Anointing of the Sick is celebrated, the priest offers the following prayer after the person has been anointed with oil:

> Father in heaven,
> through this holy anointing
> grant (name) comfort in his / her suffering.
> When he / she is afraid, give him / her courage,
> when afflicted, give him / her patience,
> when dejected, afford him / her hope,
> and when alone, assure him / her of the support of your holy people.
> We ask this through Christ our Lord.
> Amen.

Next time you are ill, offer a similar prayer to God, asking for comfort, courage, patience, hope, and support.

© Life of Jesus Mafa/www.jesusmafa.com

seem to acknowledge that there is a relationship between sin and illness. Before he heals the paralytic, he asks the scribes, "Which is easier, to say, 'Your sins are forgiven,' or to say, 'Rise and walk?'" (Matthew 9:5).

It was also believed that illness and disease were the direct result of demonic possession. Some of the Gospel accounts make this connection. Luke tells about a woman who was crippled by a spirit for eighteen years (see 13:11). In Matthew a boy is having seizures and Jesus casts a demon from him, curing him (see 17:14–18). For these reasons we probably should not see Jesus' physical healings and his **exorcisms** as two different things. They were all miracles in which Jesus restored people to both physical and spiritual wholeness at the same time. ✝

Imagine the joy that comes from being healed of a serious mental or physical illness. Why is such healing a sign of the presence of the Kingdom of God?

The Church Continues Christ's Healing Ministry

In our culture today, we see a greater connection between our spiritual health and our physical health. People are more prone to physical illness when they are feeling stressed, depressed, and yes, when they are engaged in sinful activities, such as sexual promiscuity and illegal drug use. And studies show that people of faith and prayer, people who are part of a loving family and community, often recover more quickly than those who are not.

The Church supports the work of doctors, nurses, and other medical professionals to continue the healing ministry of Christ. In fact, many of the hospitals around the world were founded by Catholic religious orders. In the United States, there are over six hundred Catholic hospitals with over 500,000 staff who treat over 5,500,000 patients a year. At most hospitals Catholic **chaplains** work with other medical professionals to care for the whole person, both body and soul. And, most important, the Sacrament of Anointing of the Sick makes Christ's healing grace available through the power of the Holy Spirit.

chaplains
Specially prepared priests to whom the spiritual care of a special group of people, such as hospital patients, military personnel, or migrants, is entrusted.

Part Review

1. What are the luminous mysteries?

2. What was the Transfiguration a sign of?

3. Describe the elites and the non-elites at the time of Jesus.

4. How are material poverty and poverty of the heart related to each other?

5. How are Adam's disobedience and Christ's obedience related?

6. How does the New Law of Christ purify our conscience?

7. What was the commandment "You shall not commit adultery" meant to teach us? What deeper insight does the New Law give us in relation to this commandment?

8. What are Christ's healings a sign of?

9. What did people in biblical times see as the causes of illness and disease?

God's Plan for Salvation Is Fulfilled

Part 1

The Suffering and Death of Jesus

God has a plan, and it was brought to fulfillment through the Passion, death, Resurrection, and Ascension of Jesus Christ, the events that are at the heart of the Paschal Mystery. They stand "at the center of the Good News that the apostles, and the Church following them, are to proclaim to the world" (*Catechism of the Catholic Church [CCC]*, 571). In previous articles we have looked at all that has led up to these central events; in this section we look more closely at them and their meaning.

We start by considering Christ's suffering and death. We should be careful not to take the meaning of these events for granted. As one person once said, "Wearing a cross on a necklace is kind of the same thing as wearing an electric chair as a piece of jewelry." How is it that we have come to revere a savior who was tried as a criminal and executed? Who are the people behind the death of Jesus, and what is the real reason he was executed? And how did his suffering and death bring us freedom from sin and death and restore us to original holiness and justice?

The topics covered in this part are:

Article 22 The Events of the Passion

Passion

The sufferings of Jesus during his final days in this life: his agony in the garden at Gethsemane, his trial, and his Crucifixion.

In AD 30 a traveling Jewish rabbi made a decision that would change the world forever. For several years he had been traveling in Galilee and Samaria, teaching, healing, and forming a band of disciples to continue his mission after his departure. Now his disciples were ready for the final challenge that lay ahead. One of them just announced that he believed the rabbi was the Messiah, the Son of the Living God. Then the rabbi—known as Jesus, son of Joseph the

A Passion Timeline

Day and Time	Event	Scripture Passages
Thursday early evening	The Last Supper	Matthew 26:20–30, Mark 14:17–26, Luke 22:14–38, John 13:1—17:26
Thursday evening	Jesus prays in the garden at Gethsemane and is soon arrested.	Matthew 26:36–56, Mark 14:32–52, Luke 22:39–53, John 18:1–13
Thursday night	Jesus faces his "trial" before the Sanhedrin. Peter denies Jesus.	Matthew 26:57–75, Mark 14:53–72, Luke 22:54–71, John 18:13–27
Friday morning (7 AM?)	Jesus faces his "trial" before Pilate and Herod.	Matthew 27:1–14, Mark 15:1–5, Luke 23:1–16, John 18:28–38
Friday morning (8 AM?)	Jesus is condemned, scourged, and led to Golgotha.	Matthew 27:15–32, Mark 15:6–21, Luke 23:18–32, John 18:38—19:16
Friday morning (9 AM?)	Jesus is crucified.	Matthew 27:33–44, Mark 15:22–32, Luke 23:33–43, John 19:17–27
Friday afternoon (3 PM?)	Jesus dies.	Matthew 27:45–56, Mark 15:33–41, Luke 23:44–49, John 19:28–37
Friday evening	Jesus is buried.	Matthew 27:57–61, Mark 15:42–47, Luke 23:50–56, John 19:38–42

carpenter—made the decision to travel to Jerusalem, where he knew he would meet his death.

Catholic life includes visual reminders of the suffering and death of Jesus. We display crucifixes, which depict the dead body of Christ—called the corpus—even though most other Christians remember Jesus with empty crosses. We have special prayer forms with visual elements—the Stations of the Cross and the mysteries of the Rosary—to help us reflect on the meaning of Jesus' death. On Good Friday we strip our churches bare to emphasize the emptiness and sorrow that Jesus and his disciples felt on that fateful day long ago.

Meeting Jesus on the way to his Crucifixion is one of the traditional seven sorrows of Mary. The feast day for Our Lady of Sorrows is on September 15.

© Pascal Deloche /Godong/Corbis

The Events Leading to Jesus' Death

Each of the four Gospels gives the same account of the events leading to Jesus' death, with small differences in details. The fact that these events are so important is evidenced by how much of each Gospel is devoted to these accounts. Even though these events represent only one day of the three years of Jesus' public ministry, they take up two of Mark's sixteen chapters. The **Passion** and Resurrection of Christ were at the center of the early Church's first preaching and teaching (see Acts 2:22–36, 3:11–15). Let us take a quick look at these events and who was involved. See the chart to find the corresponding biblical passages.

Jesus Enters Jerusalem

When Jesus decided to bring his mission to Jerusalem, things came to a head, particularly with the **chief priests.** Jerusalem was the center of Jewish faith and worship, particularly during the time of the Passover. Jesus' presence in the city was too direct a challenge to ignore. First of all, when Jesus arrived, crowds welcomed him as a triumphant king (see Matthew 21:1–11)! Next Jesus went to the Temple, the very seat of the priests' and scribes' authority, and cast out the moneychangers (see Matthew 21:12–13). He did this to protest how the chief priests and scribes had let commerce and profit become intertwined with the practice of the Jewish faith. Mark and Luke indicate that it was after this act that the religious leaders began looking for a way to kill Jesus (see Mark 11:18).

© Jozef Sedmak/Shutterstock.com

The Last Supper

Early Thursday evening Jesus gathers with his closest friends, the **Apostles,** for a final celebration of the Passover. During the meal Jesus washes their feet (see John 13:1–20) to show that true leadership is service. Because the meal is a Passover meal, Jesus identifies himself with the Paschal Lamb whose blood was shed and flesh was eaten. He does this through the institution of the Eucharist (discussed in a previous article). When we celebrate the Eucharist, we commemorate and make present Christ's sacrifice.

The Garden at Gethsemane

After the meal Jesus goes with his Apostles to one of his favorite places to pray, the garden at Gethsemane. While he is in prayer, accepting his Father's will, Judas leads the Temple guards to him so that he can be arrested and taken before the Jewish religious leaders. This sets up a wonderful biblical parallel. The first Adam disobeyed God in a garden, bringing sin and death into the world. Now Jesus, the new Adam, will make a conscious choice to obey his Father, thus defeating sin and death (see Mark 14:36). And just as Satan tempted Adam and Eve to betray God in a garden, now Satan tempts Judas to betray the Son of God in a garden (see Mark 14:43).

The Trial Before the Sanhedrin

Jesus is brought before the **Sanhedrin,** the ruling group of Jewish religious leaders. They question Jesus, and key leaders are determined to find him guilty of a capital crime. The Gospels make it clear that they have difficulty doing so (see Mark 14:55–59). The fact that it is now late at night would seem to indicate that these leaders wanted to keep this trial out of public view and get it over quickly. Because of Jesus' popularity with the non-elites, they were concerned that there would be riots if their treatment of Jesus became public. They find Jesus guilty of blasphemy when he confirms that he is the Messiah (see Mark 14:61–62). According to the Law, the penalty for blasphemy is death by stoning. However, since they are now under Roman authority, the Jewish leaders do not have the authority to condemn someone to death.

The Trial Before Pilate

As early as possible the next morning, the Jewish leaders take Jesus to the Roman governor, Pontius Pilate, and make their case against Jesus. Because Pilate does not care about Jewish religious law, they have to accuse Jesus of treason rather than blasphemy. They charge Jesus with inciting rebellion against Rome, probably of even claiming to be the king of the Jews (see Mark 15:1–3), which is a capital offense in the Roman Empire. While Luke and John indicate that Pilate thinks Jesus is innocent, the reality is that only Pilate could have ordered Jesus to be crucified. That Pilate does so indicates that he believes that Jesus' message is in some way a threat to Roman authority (see the next article, "Who Killed Jesus?"). The fact that Jesus says so little in his own defense (see Mark 15:4–5) is probably an indication that he knows he will be found guilty and that nothing he can say will change Pilate's decision.

The Scourging

Once Pilate orders Jesus' execution (some Gospels indicate that he only allows it), Jesus is prepared to be executed. A Roman execution was especially brutal. It was meant to be as horrible as possible to frighten people into obedience. First, Jesus is publicly humiliated by being clothed with a purple cloak and then crowned with thorns. This is to mock his supposed claim to be a king. Next, Jesus is scourged (whipped) with a whip that has pieces of bone and metal embedded in the leather. It was meant to tear the skin from

chief priests
These were Jewish priests of high rank in the Temple. They had administrative authority and presided over important Temple functions and were probably leaders in the Sanhedrin.

Apostles
The general term *apostle* means "one who is sent" and can be used in reference to any missionary of the Church during the New Testament period. In reference to the twelve companions chosen by Jesus, also known as "the Twelve," the term refers to those special witnesses of Jesus on whose ministry the early Church was built and whose successors are the bishops.

Sanhedrin
An assembly of Jewish religious leaders—chief priests, rabbis, scribes, and elders—who functioned as the supreme council and tribunal during the time of Christ.

a person's back. This was sometimes done to condemned prisoners to hasten their death; at times people died from this alone. Finally, he has to carry on his bloody back the crossbeam on which he will be crucified.

The Crucifixion

When Jesus reaches the hill called Golgotha, he is stripped of his clothes to completely humiliate him and is nailed through his wrists to a crossbeam, which is lifted into place on a permanent post. His arms and feet are tied to the cross to keep his body from tearing free of the nails. People who were crucified often lived for days before dying from blood loss, exposure, or the inability to breathe. The Gospels provide details that show how the events of the Crucifixion are the fulfillment of many Old Testament prophecies. Jesus' final words on the cross indicate his suffering, his humanity, his forgiveness, his love for his mother, and his trust in God.

© yasick photography/shutterstock.com

Jesus' Death

According to the Gospel accounts, Jesus dies in six hours or less, no doubt in part due to the blood he loses from the scourging. His death is accompanied by dramatic natural events: an eclipse and an earthquake (see Matthew 27:45,51). The earthquake splits the veil of the Temple, the curtain that separated the Holy of Holies from the rest of the Temple. Only the high priest could go behind the Temple veil. So the

Pray It!

The Cross Is the Power of God

Jesus,
You were obedient to your Father even though it meant that you would be abandoned by your friends, mocked by the authorities, accused of being a criminal, stripped and beaten, nailed to a cross, and executed. You remind me to do the right thing despite the difficulties I may endure. By putting all my faith in you, I know I can endure mockery, abandonment, rejection, or even worse.

Give me the strength to bear the crosses in life. In my most difficult moments, remind me that the cross is not the end, but the beginning. Give me the courage to let go of greed, hatred, lust, pride, and everything else that keeps me from doing your will. Let them die, and let me be reborn in you. In my painful moments, remind me of Saint Paul's words: "The message of the cross is foolishness to those who are perishing, but to us who are being saved it is the power of God" (1 Corinthians 1:18). Amen.

tearing of the Temple veil symbolically indicates that with the death of Christ, all people, not just the high priest, have access to the presence of God.

Normally a convicted criminal's body would have been left on the cross to be further desecrated, eaten by birds and animals. But an influential follower of Jesus was able to convince Pilate to let him take down Jesus' body and place it in his personal tomb (see Matthew 27:57–60). The Gospels are careful to mention that the location of the tomb was noted by the women disciples (see verse 61). Matthew also adds the detail that the tomb was watched by guards (see verse 66). These details confirm that Jesus' death was real and that his body was not later stolen by his followers.

Jesus' Death Is the Real Thing

Some people think that because Jesus was God, his death was no big deal for him. After all, didn't he know how it would all turn out? But the Gospel stories take great care to show that Jesus experienced doubt, pain, and fear, as he was betrayed, put through a mock trial, tortured, and crucified. He was not saved from these human feelings because of his divine nature. His death was the real thing. The Son of God died and was buried for the forgiveness of our sins so that we might experience full communion with God in this life and the next. ✝

Roman soldiers mocked Jesus because he was charged with claiming to be a king. How would the soldiers have understood the role of a king? Why did they have a hard time recognizing Jesus' kingship?

Article
23 Who Killed Jesus?

The mystery of the Incarnation tells us that Jesus was both true God and true man. So it is no surprise that there are both divine and human reasons behind the death of Jesus. To fully understand the importance of Jesus' death, we need to understand both sets of reasons. In this article we start by considering the human reasons.

The Apostles' Creed states, "[Jesus Christ] suffered under Pontius Pilate, was crucified, died and was buried." This statement tells us that a Roman governor—Pontius Pilate—was involved in Jesus' death, but it doesn't mention the Jewish religious leaders. The Gospels are clear that both Jewish and Roman leaders wanted Jesus dead. But why?

The Jewish Leaders' Reasons

For the religious leaders, the answer is fairly clear: Jesus challenged their authority to such an extent that they believed Jesus was undermining their authority with the common person. Here are some specific examples:

- **Mark 2:23—3:6.** The Pharisees and scribes taught that you could do absolutely no work on the Sabbath. Jesus' disciples plucked grain on the Sabbath, and Jesus healed on the Sabbath. Jesus challenged the Pharisees' and scribes' teaching by saying, "The sabbath was made for man, not man for the sabbath" (2:27).

- **Mark 2:1–12.** Jesus claimed to have the power to forgive sins, which the Jewish religious leaders believed was a power that belonged to God alone.

- **Luke 16:19–31.** Many of the religious leaders believed that having material wealth was a sign of being right with God. Jesus claimed that God also blessed the poor. He even taught that being rich while ignoring the poor was a sin.

- **Luke 15:1–10.** The religious leaders avoided having anything to do with common sinners such as prostitutes

Live It!

Jewish People Are Our Spiritual Brothers and Sisters

Throughout history many people have misinterpreted the Gospel accounts to conclude that all Jewish people of Jesus' time are responsible for his death. This is simply not true. We must remember that most of the early disciples, the Apostles, Jesus' mother, and even Jesus himself, were Jewish. Only the Jewish leaders who collaborated with the Roman Empire should be held accountable.

The Second Vatican Council states that "God holds the Jews most dear" and "the Church, mindful of the patrimony she shares with the Jews . . . decries hatred, persecutions, displays of anti-Semitism, directed against Jews at any time" (*Declaration on the Relation of the Church to Non-Christian Religions*, 4). Both Jews and Christians call the same God "Father"; thus, all Jewish people are our spiritual brothers and sisters.

and tax collectors. Yet Jesus freely associated with these people and chided the Pharisees for avoiding them.

As described in the article "The Events of the Passion," things came to a head when Jesus brought his mission to Jerusalem and directly confronted the authority and power of the chief priests and scribes. However, the Jewish leaders could not put Jesus to death simply because he challenged their authority. So the crime they charged him with was **blasphemy,** the crime of speaking irreverently about God (see Matthew 26:63–66). The chief priests and scribes claimed that Jesus committed blasphemy when he claimed powers for himself that belonged to God alone. According to the Law of the Old Covenant, a person could be stoned to death for this. But because they were under Roman authority, only the Roman **procurator** could order a death sentence.

The Roman Leaders' Reasons

The Roman leaders' reasons for wanting to execute Jesus are not completely clear if you just read the Gospel accounts. To understand these reasons, we need to understand how the Roman Empire stayed in power and, in particular, the role of the Roman procurator.

For all intents and purposes, the Roman procurator, or governor, held absolute power in the region he controlled. His power was enforced by the legions of soldiers under his command. The procurator was responsible to the Roman Emperor and the Roman Senate only, not to any local authorities or the local population. The procurator's main responsibilities were to send tax money regularly to Rome and to keep the peace, which generally meant stopping any rebellions against Rome. In order to help with these tasks, he sometimes appointed local people to positions of power. These local leaders were required to enforce Roman laws and collect taxes; if they did not do this, they would be quickly replaced. They were also expected to report to the procurator any suspicion they had of people plotting against Rome. In Israel at the time of Jesus, the local ruling family, the Herodians, had been cooperating with the Roman Empire for several generations. And the Herodians appointed the high priest and chief priests of the Temple, until eventually the Romans took over that too.

blasphemy
Speech or actions that show disrespect or irreverence for God; also, claiming to have the powers of God or to be God.

procurator
A word used to describe Roman governors. These men had administrative and legal authority over a province or region of the Roman Empire.

The procurator at the time of Jesus was Pontius Pilate. Why would he have ordered Jesus' Crucifixion? First, as procurator he tried everyone accused of treason against Rome and ordered the public execution of anyone he found guilty. Second, all he really needed to know is that the Jewish leaders who served him thought Jesus was a threat to Rome's authority (see Luke 23:5). We know from sources outside the Bible that Pontius Pilate was a ruthless and effective leader, responsible for the deaths of many Jewish citizens, even before Jesus' Crucifixion.

On the other hand, the Gospel accounts portray Pilate as having ambivalent feelings towards Jesus. He is amazed with Jesus' composure in facing him (Mark 15:4-5). He tested the crowd's conviction by having them choose whether to release Jesus or a criminal named Barabbas (Mark 15:6-15). In the Gospel of Luke, Pilate publicly declared Jesus innocent three times (23:4, 14, 22). But in the end, Pilate had his soldiers scourge and crucify him. Regardless of whether or not Jesus was a revolutionary, he was a threat to the peace that Pilate was pledged to maintain. The bottom line is clear; Jesus would not have been crucified without the approval of Pilate, acting on behalf of the Roman Empire. ✝

Only Pilate had the authority to condemn Jesus to death. The Gospels present him as being amazed at Jesus' composure before him.

© Brooklyn Museum/Corbis

The Irony of Jesus' Condemnations

There are at least two ironies in the human reasons behind Jesus' Passion and death. They are not specifically mentioned, but the sacred authors certainly expected their readers to see them.

The first is the crime the Jewish leaders charge Jesus with. They charge him with blasphemy, with claiming to be the Messiah, the Son of God. The irony is that Jesus is indeed the Son of God, the Second Person of the Trinity! Jesus is not committing blasphemy but is simply speaking the truth—a truth that the religious leaders of his time cannot accept.

The second is that Pilate executes Jesus in order to eliminate a threat to the authority of the Roman Empire. He wants to stop Jesus' message of a kingdom of justice with compassion for the poor, with leaders who are first servants of others. Jesus' message directly challenges the core values of the Roman Empire. The irony is that in executing Jesus, Pilate sets in motion the events bringing the Kingdom of God to its fulfillment. Pilate's actions are unable to defeat God's purpose, proving that the Kingdom of God will triumph over all earthly empires despite all their efforts to keep it from happening.

Article

24 The Meaning of the Cross

We now turn to the supernatural reasons for Jesus Christ's Passion and death. His death was not merely the execution of a subversive leader. Saint Peter, in talking about the death of Jesus, said, "This man, delivered up by the set plan and foreknowledge of God, you killed" (Acts of the Apostles 2:23). The Father planned that his Son would take on the burden of sin for all humanity, dying so that we might be free from the sentence of death. "[Christ] himself bore our sins in his body upon the cross, so that, free from sin, we might live for righteousness. By his wounds you have been healed" (1 Peter 2:24). Salvation from sin and death for every person in every age comes through the death and Resurrection of Jesus Christ.

Does all this sound too fantastic to believe? Evidently many people living at the time of Jesus thought so. Many of the speeches in the Acts of the Apostles and much of the teaching in the letters of the New Testament are devoted to explaining how Jesus' death frees us from sin. Their teaching tended to fall into three metaphors, or symbolic explanations: Jesus, the Suffering Servant; Jesus, the Paschal Lamb; and Jesus, the ransom for many. Because the symbols and the Scriptures associated with these metaphors are important in Catholic liturgy and theology, let's look at each one of them.

Jesus, the Suffering Servant

The first Christians, like Jesus himself, were Jews. Guided by the Holy Spirit, they looked to their sacred writings, the Jewish Scriptures (which contains most of the same books that are in the Old Testament) to understand the meaning of Jesus' death. No doubt they immediately thought of the "suffering servant" passages in Isaiah (42:1–4, 49:1–6, 50:4–9, and 52:13—53:12), which were discussed in the article "The Growing Messianic Hope." These passages describe an unnamed servant of the Lord who suffers greatly—not as punishment for his own sins but to save the people from theirs. "He [the suffering servant] was pierced for our transgressions, / crushed for our sins, / Upon him was the chastisement that makes us whole, / by his stripes we were healed" (Isaiah 53:5).

It is easy to see how these passages apply to the suffering and death of Jesus. In making this connection, the early Christians began to understand how Jesus' freely given obedience to the Father's will (or plan) helped to explain how we have been freed from our sins. "For just as through

Catholic Wisdom

Christ's Suffering Is a Sign of Love

Julian of Norwich, a medieval mystic, was born around 1342. To Julian, Jesus' willingness to suffer is a sign of his deep compassion and intimate care for us.

> At the same time as I saw this sight of the head bleeding, our good Lord showed a spiritual sight of his familiar love. I saw that he is to us everything which is good and comforting for our help. He is our clothing, who wraps and enfolds us for love, embraces us and shelters us, surrounds us for his love, which is so tender that he may never desert us. (*Showings*, chapter 5)

the disobedience of one person the many were made sinners, so through the obedience of one the many will be made righteous" (Romans 5:19).

© Dave Bartruff/CORBIS

One of Jesus' symbolic titles is the Lamb of God. What other symbols associated with Jesus are in this stained glass?

Jesus, the Paschal Lamb

Another event in the Old Testament that connects to Jesus' Passion is the account of the Paschal, or Passover, Lamb. This story goes all the way back to the time when the Israelites were slaves in Egypt. To convince Pharaoh to let the people go, God sent a series of ten plagues upon the Egyptian people. The last and most horrible plague was an angel of death that killed the firstborn son of every family in the land. Moses instructed the Israelites to kill a lamb and put its blood on their doorposts so the angel of death would pass over their home without killing the firstborn son. After this Pharaoh let the people go, and they began their journey to the Promised Land.

In the Gospel of John and in the Book of Revelation, Jesus is referred to as "the Lamb of God, who takes away the sin of the world" (John 1:29). To make it perfectly clear, in the Gospel of John, Jesus is crucified on the Feast of the Passover, the same day the Paschal lambs were being slaughtered in the Temple. Just as the blood of the Paschal lambs liberated the Israelites from death and slavery, so too does Jesus' death and Resurrection save all humanity from death and from slavery to sin. You will sometimes hear Christians expressing this idea with statements such as, "I've been washed in the blood of the lamb." This is why we call the mystery of Jesus' Passion, death, Resurrection, and Ascension the Paschal Mystery.

Jesus, the Ransom for Many

In the Roman Empire, a "ransom" was the price paid to release a slave. The payment was made in front of a shrine to a local god, to indicate the slave was becoming the property of that god and could no longer be owned by another person. Because they wanted to reach Gentiles (non-Jews), as well as Jews, the early Christians adapted this concept to help explain the saving nature of Jesus' death to people living in the Roman Empire. We see this particularly in the Gospel of Mark, where Jesus says, "For the Son of Man did not come to be served but to serve and to give his life a ransom for many" (10:45). The idea of ransom helps us to understand that Jesus paid to God the price of our freedom so that we are no longer "owned" by sin and death.

All these explanations are important for understanding what Catholics mean when we say Jesus died for our sins. We must be careful, though, not to interpret them too literally. If you take any of these metaphors to the extreme, God comes off as an angry and cold-hearted accountant, demanding exact payment in blood before setting us free. This is the exact opposite of Jesus' description of God as a loving and forgiving Father. What these three explanations help us to understand is that through the suffering and death of Jesus Christ, the separation between God and humanity—a consequence of the Fall—has been bridged as a result of God's initiative. This is God's great gift of love to us, the freely offered sacrifice of God himself, in the person of Jesus Christ.

A Hymn of the Cross

Saint Ephraim of Syria lived in the fourth century. He countered the Christological heresies prevalent back then through music. He composed popular hymns that taught the true faith. Ephraim was declared a Doctor of the Church in 1920. Here is a portion from one of his sermons:

> Death slew [Christ] by means of the body which he had assumed, but that same body proved to be the weapon with which he conquered death. Concealed beneath the cloak of his

manhood, his godhead engaged death in combat; but in slaying our Lord, death itself was slain. It was able to kill natural human life, but was itself killed by the life that is above the nature of man. . . .

We give glory to you, Lord, who raised up your cross to span the jaws of death like a bridge by which souls might pass from the region of the dead to the land of the living. We give glory to you who put on the body of a single mortal man and made it the source of life for every other mortal man. You are incontestably alive. Your murderers sowed your living body in the earth as farmers sow grain, but it sprang up and yielded an abundant harvest of men raised from the dead. ✝

Why Did the Father Allow His Son to Suffer?

Some people ask: "Why did the Father require his Son to die for our sins? Why didn't he find some way to save his Son from such a torturous death?" When confronted with questions like these, it is helpful to remember some of the things you have learned in these articles. First, it was not any action on the Father's part that required the Son's redeeming death. It was our first parents' Original Sin that necessitated Jesus' sacrifice. The Father allowed his Son's death in order that the power of death might be destroyed and our friendship with God restored so that we might live eternally with him.

Second, the Father did not force his Son's sacrificial death. Jesus Christ freely accepted his Passion and death. As an innocent victim, he took upon himself all the sins and injustices of humanity in order to overcome them. As the Second Person of the Trinity, Jesus' Incarnation and his death were part of his divine mission in the work of salvation. Christ's Resurrection is proof that his death was necessary to defeat the power of sin and death. The suffering and death of Christ are not signs of God's weakness but of his strength; they do not show God's apathy but show the depth of his love.

Part Review

1. When did Jesus' conflict with the chief priests come to a head? Why?

2. What dramatic events occurred at the time of Jesus' death?

3. What were the Jewish leaders' reasons for wanting Jesus to be put to death?

4. How was Jesus a threat to the Roman Empire?

5. What are three metaphors used to communicate the supernatural meaning of Jesus' death?

6. How would you answer the question, "Why would God the Father allow his Son to suffer and die as he did?"

Part 2

The Resurrection and Ascension of Jesus

God has a plan, and it was brought to fulfillment through Jesus Christ's Passion, death, Resurrection, and Ascension—the events that are at the heart of the Paschal Mystery. In these articles we focus on Christ's Resurrection and Ascension, the glorious events that are the culmination of his saving work. Without Christ's Resurrection we would have no basis to hope for our own resurrection and eternal life with God. Saint Paul claims: "If Christ has not been raised, your faith is vain; you are still in your sins. Then those who have fallen asleep in Christ have perished" (1 Corinthians 15:17–18).

But what is the Resurrection? How do we know it really happened? What is a resurrected body like? What does the Resurrection prove? Why did the resurrected Christ ascend into Heaven after forty days? The articles in this part explore these important questions. But, most important, Christ's Resurrection should cause us to rejoice because God invites us to participate in this great mystery, the culmination of his saving plan.

> For I handed on to you as of first importance what I also received: that Christ died for our sins in accordance with the scriptures; that he was buried; that he was raised on the third day in accordance with the scriptures; that he appeared to Cephas [Peter], then to the Twelve. After that, he appeared to more than five hundred brothers at once, most of whom are still living, though some have fallen asleep. (1 Corinthians 15:3–7)

The topics covered in this part are:

Article 25 The Events of the Resurrection

Throughout history there have been many great spiritual leaders: Moses, Confucius, the Buddha, and Mohammed to name a few. What makes Jesus Christ different from these other spiritual leaders? All the great spiritual leaders teach their followers to live a moral life based on love of others. Many of them also teach belief in and love for God. But only Jesus Christ is the Son of God, the Second Divine Person of the Trinity, who was raised from the dead and now reigns in Heaven forever.

The Resurrection Appearances

The four Gospels contain several accounts of the resurrected Jesus' appearing to his disciples. Because of differences in details, it is difficult to tell if some of these accounts are the same event or different events. These accounts are indicated with brackets.

Appearance	Scripture Passage
Several women (Mary Magdalene, Mary, the mother of James, Salome, and Joanna) see an angel and witness the empty tomb.	Matthew 28:1–8, Mark 16:1–8, Luke 24:1–10, John 20:1–10
Jesus appears to Mary Magdalene.	[Matthew 28:9–10], Mark 16:9, John 20:11–18
Jesus appears to two disciples walking away from Jerusalem.	Mark 16:12–13, Luke 24:13–35
Jesus commissions the eleven Apostles.	Matthew 28:16–20, Mark 16:14–18, Luke 24:36–49, [John 20:19–23]
Jesus appears to the Apostles, including Thomas.	John 20:24–29
Jesus appears to Peter and six other disciples in Galilee.	John 21:1–23
Jesus ascends to Heaven.	Mark 16:19, Luke 24:50–53, Acts 1:6–12
Jesus appears to Paul.	Acts 9:1–6

Christ's Incarnation and the **Resurrection** are closely related. He was able to save us from sin and death because he is true God and true man, the only mediator who can restore us to full communion with the Father, Son, and Holy Spirit. But the Resurrection provides the proof for this truth. Without Christ's Resurrection all our claims about who Jesus is and what he did for us sound hollow and empty. Some people have come to believe that the Resurrection never happened and have argued that it is a big hoax. But the evidence for the Resurrection is compelling.

Resurrection

The passage of Jesus from death to new life "on the third day" after his Crucifixion; the heart of the Paschal Mystery and the basis of our hope in the resurrection from the dead.

The Gospel Accounts

Each of the four Gospels has a slightly different account of what happened in the days after Jesus' death. The Gospel of Mark offers the fewest clues; it originally ended with several women discovering an empty tomb and an angel telling the women that Jesus had been raised. (A longer ending was later added to the Gospel, in which Jesus appears to Mary Magdalene and the other disciples.) In the Gospel of Matthew, Pilate places a guard at the tomb to keep the disciples from stealing Jesus' body, but an angel rolls away the stone anyway. The resurrected Jesus meets the disciples on a mountain in Galilee, where he gives them a mission to "make disciples of all nations" (Matthew 28:19). The Gospel of John takes the prize for the most Resurrection stories, with four separate accounts of Jesus' appearing to different people.

Despite their differences the Gospel stories have these points in common:

- First some women disciples, and then the men, go to the tomb and discover that the body of Jesus is no longer there.
- The women who go to the tomb find out from angels that Jesus is no longer dead but alive and will reveal himself to the disciples soon.
- Jesus reveals himself to Mary Magdalene at the tomb (and to the other Mary in Matthew).
- Later Jesus appears to groups of disciples to wish them peace and charge them with continuing his mission. Often the disciples' initial reaction is shock and fear. But soon they experience Jesus in such striking ways that they cannot doubt that it is he—alive again, and yet somehow different from the way he was before his death.

This is a painting of Mary Magdalene meeting Jesus after his Resurrection. Imagine yourself in her place. What would you be feeling at this moment?

© Life of Jesus Mafa/www.jesusmafa.com

Evidence for the Resurrection

But how do we know the Gospel accounts are all true? What if the Gospel writers simply made it all up? These are valid questions we must meet head-on if we are to be honest about what we believe. You will find that there are good arguments to show that it is reasonable to believe in the Resurrection of Jesus as a historically valid event. Let's explore some of those arguments.

One argument is that we can trust the historical validity of the New Testament books and letters. Although we do not have original copies of the New Testament books or letters, we have copies that can be traced back to within a few centuries of Jesus' earthly life. And we have lots of different ancient copies of the New Testament books and letters from different locations. When historians take these things into account, we have greater proof for the authenticity of the New Testament books than for any other ancient writing.

Another argument is that the Resurrection was a consistent belief in the early Church. You can find it in all four Gospels, in the letters of Saint Paul, and in the speeches contained in the Acts of the Apostles. In fact, experiencing the Risen Jesus was considered a key qualification for being accepted as one of the Apostles (see Acts of the Apostles

1:15–22). This is clear evidence that the earliest Christians accepted it as fact.

There is also the argument of the empty tomb. If the tomb was not empty, surely the Romans or the Jewish religious leaders would have produced the corpse right away to put to rest the rumors of Jesus' Resurrection. No evidence has been found that they tried to do this. But you might ask, "Couldn't the disciples have stolen Jesus' corpse and then claimed that he had risen?" The problem with this argument is that several of the disciples died as martyrs rather than deny their faith in the resurrected Jesus. Why would they have chosen to die for a hoax?

And we can argue that the Resurrection appearances of Jesus caused a profound change in his followers. This may be the most important evidence of all. After Jesus' death his disciples were beaten, discouraged, and afraid for their lives. Yet somehow they found the courage to go out in public and continue Jesus' mission, facing ridicule, persecution, and even death. They preached with total conviction that Jesus had risen. What other reasonable explanation could there be for this change than their encounter with the Risen Christ?

Christ's Resurrection is a real event. It is historically attested to by the disciples, who truly encountered the Risen One. The empty tomb signified that by God's power, Christ's body escaped the bonds of death. It prepared the disciples to encounter and believe in the Risen Lord.

Let's bring this to a personal level. The most important question you will ever face is this: "Do I believe that Jesus Christ was raised from the dead?" Why? Because how you answer that question will determine how seriously you live out your belief in Jesus. If you answer, "I believe in the Resurrection!" how can you not make Jesus Christ the center of your life? ☨

© Life of Jesus Mafa/www.jesusmafa.com

Article 26 What Is the Resurrection?

gnosticism
A group of heretical religious movements that claimed salvation comes from secret knowledge available only to the elite initiated in that religion.

Most people want to know what the resurrected Jesus was like. The fact that the Gospel accounts are purposefully vague gives us one clue: the resurrected Jesus cannot easily be explained in human terms. He shows up without warning and disappears just as suddenly. The disciples know he's not a ghost, because they can touch him and he eats with them. He's different enough that some people do not recognize him immediately, yet when they do recognize him, he's still the same person they knew from before. Being in Jesus' risen presence gives them peace and hope.

No one can tell you exactly what it means to be resurrected or what it will be like to experience it. This is a mystery of faith that we will fully understand only after our death. However, God does reveal to us what we need to know. You will find that chapter fifteen of Paul's First Letter to the Corinthians is the most direct biblical explanation of this question. Take a few minutes to read that chapter right now if you can. Then keep reading this article for some help in interpreting what Saint Paul is saying.

First Corinthians, Chapter Fifteen

In interpreting the meaning of First Corinthians, chapter fifteen, we have to consider what we know about literary techniques and biblical cultures. We must ask why Saint Paul wrote his letters. Clearly he wrote them to respond to specific questions or concerns that have developed in the Christian communities he is associated with. What is the question or concern Paul is addressing here? It would appear that some people in the Corinthian community have been claiming that there is no bodily resurrection from the dead. Why would they claim that with all the evidence they had for Christ's Resurrection? It is probably due to the influence of a widespread cultural belief system called **gnosticism.**

Many gnostics believed the human person is composed of two parts, body and spirit (or soul). But rather than believe that both body and spirit are good and necessary, they believed that the body is bad and the spirit is good. The body keeps the soul captive and held back from its full potential. So many gnostics believed that the goal of a full human life is to leave behind "bodily" concerns and focus primarily on the spiritual. For them, eternal life means that we will live forever as pure spirit, shedding our bodies forever. It is against this false belief that Paul is writing, to explain what resurrection truly is. He makes his argument in three steps.

First, the Resurrection really happened. In the first twelve verses of chapter fifteen, Saint Paul reminds the Corinthians that the Resurrection was a real event. He emphasizes that the Risen Christ had appeared to over five hundred believers. Notice that Paul emphasizes that Christ *appeared* rather than that people simply *saw* him. This establishes the Resurrection as an objective event, not simply a subjective event.

This information was passed on to Saint Paul from eyewitnesses, but he also had his own experience of the Risen Christ. And Saint Paul defends himself as an Apostle in

© Agnew's, London, UK/The Bridgeman Art Library International

Can you identify the three different groups near the empty tomb? Only the Gospel of Matthew has the account of guards posted at the tomb who were later paid to say that the disciples stole Jesus' body.

response to those who are attacking his credibility. By mentioning the fact that he at first persecuted the Church, he subtly suggests that it would take something pretty impressive to make him change sides. In all of this, it is implied that Christ was resurrected, body and soul, for how could human beings experience him otherwise?

Second, Christ's Resurrection is proof of our resurrection. In verses 20–24, Paul makes the point that Christ's Resurrection is the guarantee of our resurrection. He says that if we deny Christ's Resurrection, we deny any hope for our own resurrection. He goes on to say that in God's saving plan, Christ is the first to be resurrected in order that we might all be resurrected. "Since death came through a human being, the resurrection of the dead came also through a human being" (verse 21). To emphasize this Paul likens Christ's Resurrection to the "firstfruits." When the firstfruits ripen, you know that the remaining fruit will also ripen shortly and be ready for harvest.

Paul says that there is an order to God's plan: First, Christ is raised. Then all those who belong to (have faith in) Christ will be raised. When that is complete, Christ will have conquered sin and death forever and the Kingdom

Live It!

Be a Farsighted Traveler

Being nearsighted means you have trouble seeing things at a distance, or that you do not look toward the future to see what is coming. Nearsighted travelers going on a month-long jungle safari would bring things for the airplane and the hotel only. By the time they got to the main event, they would be very ill-prepared. Being a Christian means being farsighted travelers. Because of Christ's Resurrection, we know that our life does not end at death. We stay focused on our ultimate destiny, Heaven, in the following ways:

1. We pray for guidance daily.
2. We trust that following God's directions will get us to our destination, even if the road is sometimes challenging.
3. If we get detoured and end up on the wrong path, we turn around.
4. We use the road maps, the Bible and Tradition.
5. The journey continues. Our trip won't always be easy, but we have God's promise of a destination worth the cost—Heaven!

of God will be fully restored: "When everything has been subjected to him, then the Son will [also] be subjected to the one who subjected everything to him, so that God may be all in all" (verse 28). Paul concludes this section by listing all the Christian practices that would be useless if there were no resurrection.

Third, a resurrected body is a transformed body. In the third and longest section, verses 35–58, Paul attempts to explain what a resurrected body is. He can do this through analogy only. His first analogy likens our earthly body to a seed. For a seed to become what it is destined to be, it must first "die," by being buried in the ground. Only then can it grow into a plant. The plant looks nothing like the seed, but they are the same being and one is a continuation of the other. So it is with our earthly body and our resurrected body.

Though Paul cannot say exactly what a resurrected body is, he does paint us a picture of its qualities by contrasting the qualities of our earthly body with the qualities of our resurrected body.

corruptible
Something that can be spoiled or contaminated or made rotten, especially to be made morally perverted.

Earthly Body	Resurrected Body
corruptible	incorruptible
dishonorable	honorable
weak	powerful
natural body	spiritual body

When you put all these things together, the following picture emerges: Our resurrected bodies will never die, cannot be damaged by illness or disease, will not be subjected to the temptations of sin, and will not be limited by the physical constraints of time and space as we are now.

A resurrected body is not a reanimated corpse. Jesus was truly transformed by the Resurrection, just as we will be after our death. At our death our soul will live on, and at the end of the world, God will join our soul to our resurrected body. We will still be the same person, but we will have an

Mary Magdalene

Mary Magdalene, or Mary of Magdala (Magdalene indicates she was from the town of Magdala), is among the first and greatest saints who lived in the company of Jesus. Yet she came from a very troubled past. We are told that Jesus cast out seven demons from her (see Mark 16:9, Luke 8:2), suggesting she had suffered from severe physical and emotional illnesses. After her healing she became one of Jesus' disciples, following him from village to village where he proclaimed the Good News of the Kingdom (see Luke 8:1–2, Mark 15:40–41).

Mary Magdalene had courage. She was present at the cross when most of the men who followed Jesus had all run away (see John 19:25). At daybreak on the day of Jesus' Resurrection, Mary, with Mary the mother of James, went to the tomb where Jesus had been buried. On seeing the empty tomb, they were fearful yet overjoyed. As they hurried to tell the other disciples, Jesus met them and greeted them, "Do not be afraid" (Matthew 28:10). (See Matthew 28:1–10, Mark 16:1–10, Luke 24:1–12, John 20:1–18.)

Put yourself in Mary's place as she recognized the Risen Christ. Can you imagine the surprise, the joy, the awe she must have felt? Make Mary Magdalene your model of courage and trust as you follow Jesus.

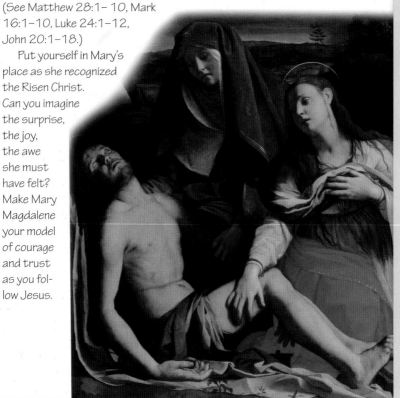

utterly new kind of existence. Beyond that we cannot say much more, but we can trust that it will be truly glorious and wonderful! ✝

Article

27 The Significance of Christ's Resurrection

Why do we naturally root for the good guys to win in books and movies? Why does it sicken and sadden us when someone dies tragically or at a young age? Why do medical professionals work so tirelessly to save people with a life-threatening illness or disease? The answer is a simple one. God created us for eternal life—a life in which there is no hatred, pain, or injustice. Even many people who do not believe in God do not easily accept dying and death.

In the previous articles, we have touched on the religious significance of Christ's Resurrection. In this article we look more closely at this, identifying those things that are confirmed by Christ's Resurrection and what the Resurrection makes possible for us.

The Resurrection Confirms Revealed Truths

Many things that were revealed by God become crystal clear because of the Resurrection. The following are some of those things.

Jesus Is the Son of God

For the first disciples, seeing the resurrected Jesus was clear proof that Jesus was more than just another human being. Jesus himself predicted this in the Gospel of John: "When you lift up the Son of Man, then you will realize that I AM" (8:28). The story of doubting Thomas says it very clearly. When Thomas sees the resurrected Jesus for the first time, he declares, "My Lord and my God!" (20:28). Belief in Jesus' Resurrection

Can you identify with the doubts of Thomas the Apostle? Remember he was also one of the first to declare Jesus' divinity (John 20:28).

© Scala/Art Resource, NY

and belief in the Incarnation go hand in hand. Throughout the centuries people have believed in the divinity of Jesus Christ because they first believed in his Resurrection.

All Jesus' Teachings Are True

If the Resurrection reveals the truth of Jesus' divinity, then it also reveals that all his other teachings are true. If we believe that Jesus was raised from the dead, how can we not also believe that Jesus spoke the truth in . . .

- claiming that God's love for us has no limits
- claiming that we find fulfillment only by first loving and serving God and then by loving and serving others
- claiming that forgiveness is more powerful and God-like than revenge
- teaching that the rich must share with the poor
- teaching that we must refuse to accept the human-made prejudices that separate us from one another

Pray It!

Life after Death

Death leads to new life. Jesus even uses the natural world to demonstrate this point: "I say to you, unless a grain of wheat falls to the ground and dies, it remains just a grain of wheat; but if it dies, it produces much fruit" (John 12:24). We experience many smaller deaths before we reach the end of our lives: graduation marks the end of an era, friendships end, we outgrow our youthful dreams, our innocence dies after learning some family secret, or maybe our romantic interests get crushed. In the midst of suffering and loss, it is sometimes difficult to see resurrection ahead. So we pray:

Lord Jesus,
Most of your friends left you.
You were falsely accused of a crime;
And you were beaten and humiliated in public.
Yet you trusted that your Father would make all things right.
Give me the courage to trust you.
Remind me that beyond the small deaths I experience,
There is resurrection,
There is new life.
There is the joy and happiness that you alone provide.
Amen.

The Resurrection is a guarantee that all these things—and many other things Jesus taught that are not on this list—are true beyond a doubt.

exegesis
The study and proper interpretation of the Scriptures.

The Resurrection Opens the Way to New Life

> The Paschal Mystery has two aspects: by his death, Christ liberates us from sin; by his Resurrection, he opens for us the way to new life. This new life is above all justification that reinstates us in God's grace, "so that as Christ was raised from the dead by the glory of the Father, we too might walk in the newness of life."[1] (*CCC*, 654)

Christ's Resurrection does more than just confirm the truths he taught and the claim that he is the Son of God. His Resurrection "is the principle and source of our future resurrection" (*CCC*, 655). Because of the Resurrection, death is not the end; it is the doorway into new and eternal life in full communion with God and with one another. We know that the life we live now is not all there is, as some people claim. We live in hope because the Risen Christ lives in our hearts. The sufferings and pain of this life can be endured because we know that something better and glorious is yet to come.

Saint Melito of Sardis lived in the second century. He was bishop of Sardis and was known for his biblical **exegesis** and theological writings. Most of his writings have been lost, but we do have some of his sermons. In his Easter sermon, he portrays Christ speaking for himself about the triumph of the Resurrection. Here is an excerpt:

After his Resurrection Jesus judges those who died before his coming, sending them to either Heaven or Hell.

© Erich Lessing/Art Resource, NY

> I have destroyed death, triumphed over the enemy, trampled Hell underfoot, bound the strong one, and taken men up to the heights of Heaven: I am the Christ. Come, then, all you nations of men, receive forgiveness for the sins that defile you. I am your forgiveness. I am the Passover that brings salvation. I am the lamb who was immolated for you. I

The Resurrection Is the Work of the Holy Trinity

Study this image of the resurrected Christ and recall what you know about symbols and signs that are used to signify the presence of the Father and the Holy Spirit. Do you see any of those in this image? The Resurrection is the work of all three Divine Persons of the Holy Trinity. We sometimes signify this by saying that the Father raised up his Son (see Acts of the Apostles 2:24, Romans 6:4). But the Son was not just a passive participant. In the Gospel of John, Jesus says: "No one takes it [his life] from me, but I lay it down on my own. I have power to lay it down, and power to take it up again" (10:18). And wherever the Father and the Son are at work, there you will also find the Holy Spirit at work.

am your ransom, your life, your resurrection, your light; I am your salvation and your king. I will bring you to the heights of Heaven. With my own right hand I will raise you up, and I will show you the eternal Father. ✝

Article 28 The Ascension

After the Resurrection the appearances of the resurrected Jesus continue for a period of forty days. During this time the Scriptures indicate that Jesus did two things: he taught his disciples how to interpret the Scriptures in relation to his life, death, and Resurrection (see Luke 24:44–48), and he directed them to continue his mission: "Go, therefore, and make disciples of all nations, baptizing them in the name of the Father, and of the Son, and of the holy Spirit, teaching them to observe all that I have commanded you. And behold, I am with you always, until the end of the age" (Matthew 28:19–20). And then Jesus left them. Or did he?

In this article, besides looking more closely at the Ascension, we look at a related event: Christ's descent into Hell.

Christ's Descent into Hell

After his death and before his Resurrection, Jesus Christ descended into Hell. There is a passing reference to this in the Letter to the Ephesians, which says: "What does 'he ascended' mean except that he also descended into the lower (regions) of the earth? The one who descended is also the one who ascended far above all the heavens, that he might fill all things" (4:9–10). This means that Jesus experienced death as completely as we do. He too experienced the complete loss of physical life that comes with death.

It also means that after his death, Jesus went to the realm of the dead, where the souls of all those who had died before him awaited his judgment. The Scriptures call the realm of the dead "Hell," which is *Sheol* in Hebrew and *Hades* in Greek. Hell is essentially the absence of God. Those who are **righteous** are brought into Heaven, and the unrighteous are condemned to remain in Hell, separated from God for all eternity.

righteous
To be sinless and without guilt before God. Can also be used as a noun

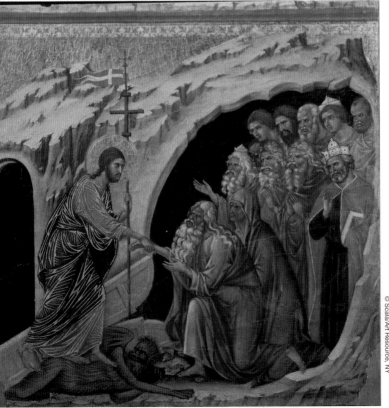

This image of Jesus' descent into the world of the dead is filled with symbols. Who has he crushed? Who has been waiting for his arrival?

© Scala/Art Resource, NY

Ascension

The "going up" into Heaven of the Risen Christ forty days after his Resurrection.

The immediate implication of Christ's descent into Hell is that he brought salvation to all the righteous souls who died before his own Resurrection. But the full significance is that Christ's death and Resurrection will bring salvation to the righteous of all times and all places. By descending into Hell, Jesus completely established his power over all creation—on earth, in Heaven, and in Hell.

Christ's Ascension

We proclaim the truth of the **Ascension** in this phrase of the Nicene Creed: "He ascended into Heaven and is seated at the right hand of the Father." The Gospel authors had a hard time putting this event into words. Matthew and John do not mention it at all. In Mark it simply says, "So then the Lord Jesus, after he spoke to them, was taken up into heaven and took his seat at the right hand of God" (16:19). Luke says, "As he blessed them he parted from them and was taken up to heaven" (24:51). The author of Luke continues with a slightly longer version of the Ascension at the beginning of Acts of the Apostles (see 1:6–12).

These Gospel accounts are trying to describe an event that is beyond human comprehension. Many people in the ancient world believed that a layer of water covered the sky and was the physical boundary of the universe. Once you got past those waters, you were in Heaven. So it made sense to think that if Jesus were joining his Father in Heaven, he would have to rise into the sky and travel past the waters. Today we know that there is no layer of water over the sky and that

© Réunion des Musées Nationaux / Art Resource, NY

Mary and the Apostles witness Jesus' Ascension into Heaven. Notice the variety of reactions.

Going Up!

In the Scriptures, approaching *God* is often associated with ascending, or going up to a high place. Jesus ascends into Heaven and descends into Hell. Solomon built the Temple on the highest hilltop in Jerusalem. Psalm 24 says, "Who may go up the mountain of the LORD? / Who can stand in his holy place?" (verse 3). The prophets frequently speak of God's "holy mountain." The prophet Elijah encountered God in a tiny whispering sound on a mountain.

We know, of course, that God is present everywhere and that *up* and *down* are relative terms. So why might the Bible associate God's presence with ascending to high places? One reason is that high places are more visible and that God seeks to be known by all people. Jesus said, "A city set on a mountain cannot be hidden" (Matthew 5:14). Another possible reason is that going uphill takes more work than going downhill. So approaching God takes some effort; it is not always the easiest path. Can you think of any other reasons why going up to a high place is associated with God's presence?

Heaven doesn't lie just outside our atmosphere. However, that doesn't change the reality the Gospel writers were trying to address: that after spending time with some of his faithful followers after his Resurrection, Jesus left this world to be with his Father in Heaven. We will explore the reasons for this in the next article. For now it is enough to say that Jesus left this world to open wide Heaven's doors for us and to actually be more present to us through the power of the Holy Spirit. ✝

Article 29 The Significance of Christ's Ascension

We celebrate Christ's Ascension forty days after Easter. Because the date for Easter varies from year to year, so does the date of the Feast of the Ascension. It always falls on a Thursday, but in many dioceses it is celebrated on the following Sunday. Some Catholics do not see the need for celebrating the Ascension. Most likely this is because they do not understand its importance. But Christ's Ascension is a

symmetry
When the opposite ends of an equation or an event balance each other or have similar properties or characteristics.

paradox
A statement that seems contradictory or opposed to common sense and yet is true.

very important part of God's plan of salvation, and once you understand it, you will want to celebrate it every year!

The Ascension Reveals Christ's Glory

We have already shown that the Incarnation and the Resurrection are closely linked. Similarly, the Incarnation and the Ascension are also closely linked. These two events form a kind of **symmetry.** In the Incarnation the Son of God leaves Heaven to come to earth, where he humbly assumes a human nature. In the Ascension the Son of God leaves earth to return to Heaven, where his full glory is revealed. But here's the amazing thing. Jesus Christ did not leave his human nature behind when he returned to Heaven. For the rest of eternity, he remains true God and true man. The following are three implications of this great mystery.

First, it means that Jesus Christ now has full authority over Heaven, earth, and even Hell. He is now free from the limits he humbly accepted during his time on earth. This is signified by the fact that he is seated at the right hand of the Father. He has demonstrated his authority by his descent into Hell, his Resurrection from the dead, and his Ascension into Heaven. The respect we should have for him is expressed in an early Christian hymn quoted by Saint Paul: "At the name of Jesus \ every knee should bend, \ of those in heaven and on earth and under the earth, \ and every tongue confess that \ Jesus Christ is Lord" (Philippians 2:10–11).

Second, the Ascension means that all humanity now has the possibility of spending eternity with God in Heaven. After his Ascension into Heaven, Jesus remains fully God and fully man—he does not give up his human nature even though his mission has been accomplished. Thus he honors our human nature and has opened the doors to Heaven

Catholic Wisdom

Here He Is

In his book *The Confessions*, Saint Augustine reflects on the Ascension of Christ. He writes: "He left our sight so that we might return to our heart, and there find him there. He went away and look: here he is." If the Risen Christ never ascended into Heaven, we would look for him outside ourselves rather than recognize him in our heart. We would look for a person rather than find him in everyone we meet.

for all humanity, overcoming the final barriers separating humanity from God. In Heaven Jesus' resurrected body assumes its full glory, as will ours.

Third, it means that in a **paradoxical** way, by leaving the earth physically, Jesus can be more present to us now than before his Ascension. Before his final Ascension, Jesus is still somehow limited by time and space. This seems to be indicated by Jesus' mysterious words to Mary Magdalene, "Stop holding on to me, for I have not yet ascended to the Father" (John 20:17).

Jesus' presence to us, even after his Ascension, is connected to two promises he made in the Gospels. His very last words in the Gospel of Matthew are, "And behold, I am with you always, until the end of the age" (28:20). His second promise was to send the Holy Spirit: "And I will ask the Father, and he will give you another Advocate to be with you always, the Spirit of truth, which the world cannot accept, because it neither sees nor knows it. But you know it, because it remains with you, and will be in you. I will not leave you orphans; I will come to you" (John 14:16–18). By sending his Spirit, Jesus is now with us in a new way. From the beginning until the end of time, the mission of the Son and the Spirit is linked and inseparable; whenever one is sent, the other is also present.

The Ascension: A Visual Meditation

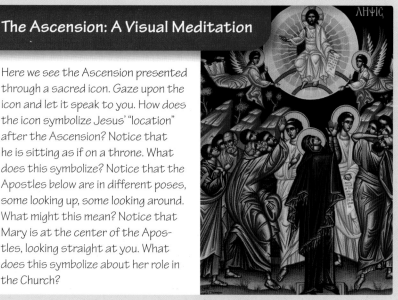

Here we see the Ascension presented through a sacred icon. Gaze upon the icon and let it speak to you. How does the icon symbolize Jesus' "location" after the Ascension? Notice that he is sitting as if on a throne. What does this symbolize? Notice that the Apostles below are in different poses, some looking up, some looking around. What might this mean? Notice that Mary is at the center of the Apostles, looking straight at you. What does this symbolize about her role in the Church?

So Jesus never really left us even though he ascended into Heaven. How is he present to us now? First and foremost he is present to us in the Sacrament of the Eucharist, in his sacred Body and Blood. But he is also present to us in the Scriptures, in our private prayer, in the liturgy, through our friends and family, and in our service to others. After his Ascension, Jesus is no longer limited to being in one place at one particular time. He is free to be everywhere, with everyone, for all time. ✝

Part Review

1. Describe several of Jesus' Resurrection appearances.

2. Give one argument for believing in the Resurrection as a historically validated event.

3. What question or concern was Saint Paul addressing in First Corinthians, chapter fifteen?

4. How will our resurrected body be different from our earthly body?

5. What revealed truths are confirmed by the Resurrection?

6. Why does Christ's Resurrection give us hope for our own resurrection?

7. Why did Christ have to descend into Hell?

8. Describe three things that are results of Christ's Ascension.

Part 3

Redeemed by Christ: Our Eternal Destiny

God has a plan, and you are a part of it! We have been saying this throughout this book, and it probably strikes each of you differently. Some of you might be thinking, "Of course, that's obvious." Others might be thinking, "That's a nice thought, but it really doesn't affect my daily life in any meaningful way." And still others might be thinking, "What are you talking about?"

The reality is that the Paschal Mystery has everything to do with you and your life. Christ suffered, died, was buried, and rose so that you might be saved from sin and saved for a full and glorious life, both now and for all eternity. God wants you to accept this truth and base your life on it; this is the most important choice you will face throughout your life. The remaining articles explore what this means for you, how to live your life with Christ. In particular, the articles in this part look at what we are saved *from* and what we are saved *for.*

The topics covered in this part are:

- Article 30: "Saved from . . ." (page 132)

- Article 31: "Saved for . . ." (page 134)

- Article 32: "Our Judgment by God" (page 139)

- Article 33: "Heaven, Hell, and Purgatory" (page 143)

Article 30 Saved from . . .

Saint Augustine is famous for many things, but one theme stands out in many of his writings: the human desire for God. Augustine is famous for saying, "You have made us for yourself, O Lord, and our heart is restless until it rests in you." Here is an excerpt from one of his writings on this topic:

> The entire life of a good Christian is in fact an exercise of holy desire. You do not yet see what you long for, but the very act of desiring prepares you, so that when he comes you may see and be utterly satisfied. . . . By desiring Heaven we exercise the powers of our soul. Now this exercise will be effective only to the extent that we free ourselves from desires leading to infatuation with this world. Let me return to the example I have already used, of filling an empty container. God means to fill each of you with what is good; so cast out what is bad! If he wishes to fill you with honey and you are full of sour wine, where is the honey to go? The vessel must be emptied of its contents and then be cleansed. Yes, it must be cleansed even if you have to work hard and scour it. It must be made fit for the new thing, whatever it may be. (From the *Tractates on the First Letter of John*)

The source of Saint Augustine's inspiration is symbolized in his painting. His mind is influenced by God's truth *(veritas)* and by compassion (his heart).

Augustine's words remind us that through the Paschal Mystery, Christ is saving us *from* something and he is also saving us *for* something. We need to be saved from the things that fill our lives with lies and empty promises. We must allow Christ to "empty" our lives of these things. In this article we look more closely at some of the things the Paschal Mystery saves us *from*. In the next article, we look at those things we are being saved *for*.

Saved from Sin and the Consequences of Sin

So what do we need to be saved from? Human history, the stories you hear in books, songs, and movies, and your own experiences testify that sin is the most fundamental thing we need to be saved from. We all sin, and every time we do, our relationship with God is damaged. What's more, we are unable to keep from sinning on our own power; we need God's grace to save us from sin. The Paschal Mystery saves us from both Original Sin and personal sin and from the following negative consequences of sin:

- **Guilt and shame.** Sin causes us to feel guilt and shame. Some people don't recognize that they are feeling guilty or shameful; they just know they are feeling bad. Others deny or repress those feelings because they do not want to face them. Unless we deal directly with these feelings through our honest sorrow and repentance in the Sacrament of Penance and Reconciliation, they will do further damage to us. We will eventually feel depressed and unlovable, unable to experience the love and communion God has waiting for us.

- **Loneliness, despair, and the feeling of being unloved.** It is natural to feel lonely at times, especially when we are separated from close friends and family members. But there is a deeper loneliness that we experience, caused by the shame that is the result of sin. Shame causes us to doubt our own goodness; we forget that we are made in the image of God. We fall into despair and start to believe that no one could love us—neither God nor other people. We end up isolated, separated from God and from the people who would love us. We can feel this kind of loneliness and despair even in a crowd of friendly people.

- **Addictions and attachment to things.** When we feel guilt and shame, when we feel lonely and unloved, we look for ways to ease these negative and painful feelings. One way many people try to do this is by using things that bring us a momentary high: alcohol, drugs, sex, and even television, gaming, or food. These can easily lead to obsessive behaviors or active addictions. Another way we try to ease the pain is by accumulating money and things, believing we can buy our way back to happiness. All these things are dead ends. They do not deal with the real problem: our separation from God caused by Original Sin and our own personal sin.

- **Death.** "For the wages of sin is death" (Romans 6:23). Death is the ultimate separation from God, the natural outcome of Original Sin and our personal sins. But for those who have been baptized, live a life of faith, and die free of mortal sin, physical death is but a passing over into new and eternal life because of the Paschal Mystery. For those who do not accept God's grace, physical death is the beginning of eternal separation from God, who is the source of all love and goodness.

✝

Article

31 Saved for . . .

Christ's Passion, death, Resurrection, and Ascension do not just save us from bad things. In fact, sometimes Christians focus too much on these things and can come across as very somber and unhappy people. The stronger focus of the Paschal Mystery should be on what we are saved for: a new and glorious life in loving communion with God and one another. This article picks up where the previous article left off—reflecting on the wonderful life of union with Christ that he has saved us for!

Resurrection in the Old Testament

It may surprise you to know that the Old Testament books rarely make reference to an afterlife. In the Book of Ecclesiastes we read, "The dead no longer know anything. There is no further recompense for them, because all memory of them is lost" (9:5). This suggests that a common view among many of Jesus' ancestors was that there was nothingness after death. Nevertheless, there is also evidence that a nascent concept of life after death emerged among the Jewish people. We know this because two of the last Old Testament books to be written—a couple of centuries before the birth of Jesus— contain references to life after death (see 2 Maccabees 7:23, Daniel 12:1–3).

The Paschal Mystery Saves Us for Eternal Life

So what does the Paschal Mystery save us for? Ultimately we are saved for eternal life, to live in full communion with God in Heaven. But the process begins in this life, as we are also saved from sin and its effects. The things we are saved for are in many ways the opposite of what we are saved from. Christ "empties" us from sin, shame, loneliness, despair, and unhealthy attachments so that he can "fill us" with his wonderful presence.

Saints and Joy

An understanding that might need correction is our image of the saints. Most often we picture them with a very serious, if not grim, demeanor. So it can be excused if you think of them as somber, serious individuals who never had a good belly laugh. But you would probably be wrong.

A true saint is a happy, joyful person. The poetry of Francis of Assisi reveals the great joy he found in life: "The tree of love its roots hath spread \ Deep in my heart, and rears its head; \ Rich are its fruits: they joy dispense; \ Transport the heart, and ravish sense." The large but brilliant Thomas Aquinas was nicknamed "dumb ox," surely a sign that he had a good sense of humor. Thérèse of Lisieux once expressed her joy even in suffering by saying: "I will sing even when I must pick my flowers amid thorns. The longer and sharper the thorns are, the sweeter my song will sound." Make no mistake, most saints were not glum or sour individuals; they were happy and joyful people who found delight in all their relationships.

venial sin

A less serious offense against the will of God that diminishes one's personal character and weakens but does not rupture one's relationship with God.

mortal sin

An action so contrary to the will of God that it results in complete separation from God and his grace. As a consequence of that separation, the person is condemned to eternal death. For a sin to be a mortal sin, three conditions must be met: the act must involve grave matter, the person must have full knowledge of the evil of the act, and the person must give his or her full consent in committing the act.

beatific vision

Directly encountering and seeing God in the glory of Heaven.

What things in your life keep you captive, keep you from experiencing a life full of forgiveness, freedom, joy, and love?

- **Forgiveness and healing.** Our life with Christ is marked by the forgiveness of sins. In the Gospels, Jesus is constantly teaching about the importance of forgiveness. In fact, there are times when people come to him for physical healing, but he first focuses his attention on forgiving their sins. Christ's teaching and example is the reason why the forgiveness of sins is so central to the sacramental life of the Church. In Baptism the mark of Original Sin is removed and our personal sins are forgiven. The Eucharist wipes away **venial sins** and preserves us from future **mortal sins.** The Sacrament of Penance and Reconciliation frees us from all personal sins, both venial and mortal. Hopefully you have known the joy and the freedom that come from being forgiven and from forgiving others.

- **Freedom.** "For freedom Christ set us free; so stand firm and do not submit again to the yoke of slavery" (Galatians 5:1). Paul is not talking about being enslaved to other people. He is teaching us that through the Paschal Mystery, Christ sets us free from all things that enslave us. We are freed from the guilt and shame of sin. We are freed from despair and feeling unlovable. We are freed from attachment to things, which brings us false joy. We are freed from the fear of God's punishment and death. We are free to experience all the joy and love God wants us to have.

© osari/istockphoto.com

- **Joy.** "For the kingdom of God is not a matter of food and drink, but of righteousness, peace, and joy in the holy Spirit" (Romans 14:17). The great Christian author C. S. Lewis wrote a book titled *Surprised by Joy*. In the book Lewis tells of his journey from being an atheist to being a fully committed Christian. He tells how his whole life was a search for joy and that he never truly found it until he accepted the source of all joy: God. Lewis discovered what you hopefully know already—that our life in Christ is a joyful life because we have been freed from those things that separate us from God and we are now filled with the love of God. That is why saints still have joy in situations that many people would find painful and disheartening.

- **Loving communion.** "The love of God has been poured out into our hearts through the holy Spirit that has been given to us" (Romans 5:5). Christ suffered, died, was resurrected, and ascended into Heaven so that our original holiness and justice that had been lost through Adam's sin would be restored. No longer are we separated from God, one another, and creation by Original Sin. Baptism restores our ability to experience the full measure of God's love and friendship. In this earthly life, we experience that only in partial ways, although at times the veil is somewhat lifted and we may experience a glimpse of the **beatific vision** the saints enjoy in Heaven.

- **Eternal life.** "Amen, I say to you, there is no one who has given up house or wife or brothers or parents or children for the sake of the kingdom of God who will not receive [back] an overabundant return in this present age and eternal life in the age to come" (Luke 18:30). Ultimately, the Passion, death, Resurrection, and Ascension of Christ save us for eternal life in Heaven. There we will enjoy the beatific vision; that is, we will be in full communion with the Holy Trinity and we will know God face-to-face. Words cannot describe what this will be like, but the Book of Revelation gives us a hint: "God's dwelling is with the human race. He will dwell with them and they will be his people and God himself will always be with them [as their God]. He will wipe every tear from their eyes, and there shall be no more death or mourning, wailing or pain, [for] the old order has passed away" (21:3–4).

We Already Share in Christ's Death and Resurrection

All salvation comes from Jesus Christ, the Head, through the Church, which is his Body. Our salvation depends on our faith in Christ and on the Church. Through Baptism we enter the Church and become participants in Christ's death and Resurrection. We are on our journey to salvation. In the waters of Baptism, we die to sin and are raised to new life in Christ. This means all our sins are forgiven by God and the consequences erased, including Original Sin and our personal sins. Nothing remains to keep us from entering the Kingdom of Heaven. Nothing separates us from God. We are a "new creation," an adopted child of God, and we "share in the divine nature" (2 Corinthians 5:17, 2 Peter 1:4).

Yet obstacles remain for us. Though the mark of Original Sin has been removed from our souls, its effects linger; we experience weakness of will, we are affected by illness and other frailties, and we are still tempted to sin. The inclination to sin is called concupiscence. And though we are a new creation, we will not have our resurrected bodies until after

Live It!

Our Weakness Is Our Strength

"For I do not do what I want, but I do what I hate" (Romans 7:15). Saint Paul is describing the guilt we feel after doing something wrong. Afterwards we ask, "Why did I do it?" Sometimes we make things worse by avoiding responsibility and blaming others, but Christ calls us to a higher path. We must admit our sin and examine our weakness. Ask yourself: "Did I do it because I'm lonely and want others to like me? because I did not want to look scared? because I feel empty inside?" Answering these questions can be painful because we must face the dark places in ourselves that we need to be saved from.

Paul later writes that the Spirit "comes to the aid of our weakness" (Romans 8:26). Our weakness is what makes us reach out to God and rely on him alone. Reaching out to God and relying on his grace instead of our power is what makes us strong. Because Saint Paul knew this, he could say, "For when I am weak, then I am strong" (2 Corinthians 12:10).

our death. We are in a kind of in-between state, which some have called the "already but not yet" time. We are already citizens of the Kingdom of God, but we are not yet in a state of perfect grace.

So, between our Baptism and our death, each of us is on a journey to become "perfect, just as your heavenly Father is perfect" (Matthew 5:48). To assist us on this journey, at Baptism we receive the gift of **sanctifying grace.** This grace enables us to practice the **theological virtues:** to have complete faith in God, to put all our hope in God, and to love God with all our strength. It also helps us to follow the lead of the Holy Spirit in our lives by using the gifts of the Holy Spirit. And it helps us to grow in goodness by living out the moral virtues. The Sacraments of the Church aid us on our journey toward Heaven, starting with Baptism. ✝

sanctifying grace
The grace that heals our human nature wounded by sin and restores us to friendship with God by giving us a share in the divine life of the Trinity. It is a supernatural gift of God, infused into our souls by the Holy Spirit, that continues the work of making us holy.

theological virtues
The name for the God-given virtues of faith, hope, and love. These virtues enable us to know God as God and lead us to union with him in mind and heart.

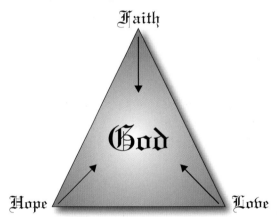

Article
32 Our Judgment by God

As a student you are used to being tested and judged. You have tests or assessments in all of your classes. You may have to be judged in order to qualify for a team or a play. So it is not a surprising thing if the thought of being tested or judged does not excite you. Being judged is not most people's idea of a good time. Let's keep in mind, though, that the one judgment that really counts—the one that should be our ultimate concern—is our judgment by Christ at the end of our lives. He does not want us to fear this judgment, but he does call us to prepare for it with the utmost seriousness. Saint

John of the Cross says reassuringly, "At the evening of life, you shall be examined in love."

Our Particular Judgment

The New Testament reveals that each of us will face two times of judgment: our particular judgment and the Final Judgment. Immediately after death each person undergoes the personal, particular judgment by Christ. Our souls will be rewarded according to our faith and works. The story of the rich man and Lazarus (see Luke 16:19–31) and the words of Christ to the repentant thief (see 23:43) affirm this immediate judgment that determines our souls' ultimate destiny: Heaven or Hell.

So if the particular judgment is kind of like our life's final exam, what is it that we will be judged on? Because the Gospel of John talks about eternal life more than any of the other Gospels, it is helpful to consider what Jesus says in John about the requirements for inheriting eternal life:

- Believe in the Son of Man, God's only Son (see 3:15–16).
- Obey Jesus (see 3:36).
- Hear Jesus and believe the One who sent him (see 5:24, 17:3).
- Eat Jesus' flesh and drink his blood (see 6:54).
- Don't be attached to the things of this world (see 12:25).

In addition to these things, we should also consider Jesus' description of the Last Judgment in Matthew 25:31–46. In this passage Jesus says that those who will inherit Heaven

Catholic Wisdom

A Few Saints Speak about Death

"I am not dying; I am entering life." (Saint Thérèse of Lisieux)

"For even dead, we are not at all separated from one another, because we all run the same course and we will find one another again in the same place." (Saint Simeon of Thessalonica)

"Death is nothing except going back to him, where he is, and where we belong." (Blessed Teresa of Calcutta)

Who Can Be Saved?

The Church has always taught that the Sacrament of Baptism is necessary for our salvation. Jesus himself says this in the Gospel of John: "Amen, amen, I say to you, no one can enter the kingdom of God without being born of water and Spirit" (John 3:5). Does this mean that people in non-Christian religions, who have been raised in them all their lives and have never heard the truth of Christ presented in a convincing way, will all go to Hell?

Such a statement would be contrary to God's mercy and love. That is why the *Catechism of the Catholic Church* teaches that "every man who is ignorant of the Gospel of Christ and of his Church, but seeks the truth and does the will of God in accordance with his understanding of it, can be saved. It may be supposed that such persons would have *desired Baptism explicitly* if they had known its necessity" (1260). This is why it is sometimes said that non-Christians can be saved through the Baptism of desire.

are those who fed the hungry, gave drink to the thirsty, welcomed strangers, clothed the naked, cared for the ill, and visited those who were in prison.

The Final Judgment

We call the time when Christ returns in his glory and all the dead will be raised "the last day" or "the Final Judgment." Saint Paul tries to explain that moment in the First Letter to the Thessalonians:

> Indeed, we tell you this, on the word of the Lord, that we who are alive, who are left until the coming of the Lord, will surely not precede those who have fallen asleep. For the Lord himself, with a word of command, with the voice of an archangel call and with the trumpet of God, will come down from heaven, and the dead in Christ will rise first. Then we who are alive, who are left, will be caught up together with them in the clouds to meet the Lord in the air. Thus we shall always be with the Lord. (4:15–17)

Jesus himself foretold of his coming again in Gospel passages such as Mark 13:24–27: "Then they will see 'the Son of Man coming in the clouds' with great power and glory" (verse 26). This event is called the second coming, or a more Catholic term, Christ's Parousia, a Greek word meaning "arrival." The Parousia will signal a final judgment of all humanity.

Matthew 25:31–46 is the clearest biblical teaching we have about the Final Judgment. This passage tells how Jesus will gather all humanity together to face a final judgment. Acting as supreme judge, Christ will reveal the secret character of each person's heart. He will separate those who have followed his will by caring for others, from those who did not follow his will because they lived only for themselves. Every person will be held accountable for his or her own deeds. Those who followed the will of God and accepted his grace will be welcomed into his eternal, heavenly Kingdom, prepared for them from the beginning of the world. Those who refused his grace and failed to serve Christ in needy and suffering people will be sent into eternal punishment.

Thus at the end of time, the Kingdom of God will come into its perfection. The Book of Revelation teaches that at that time all creation will be transformed, and there will be "a new heaven and a new earth" (21:1). The just will reign with God in Heaven for eternity, their souls united with their glorified,

This image of the final judgment is based on Matthew 25:31–46. What do you think the artist is trying to communicate to those who view this painting?

© Walraf Richartz Museum/The Bridgeman Art Library

resurrected bodies. God will be all in all because the whole of creation will be in perfect communion with its creator.

When Will Christ Return?

Jesus Christ did not return for the Final Judgment during Paul's lifetime. Throughout the centuries that followed, the Church has pondered the question "When will Christ return again?" And the answer has always been this: only God knows the time. Human history could well go on for thousands or millions of years. Or Christ could return tomorrow. Some Christian leaders have tried to predict the time of the second coming, but Catholics have learned from the first Christians that every effort to do so misses the real point of this teaching—that we should live every day like it could be our last.

It was mentioned at the beginning of this article, and it is worth repeating again at the end, that Christ does not want us to fear his judgment. He wants us to trust his love and his mercy and then to follow him as completely as we can. If we do this, we have nothing to fear. We do not save ourselves; it is only through the love, mercy, and power of the Holy Trinity that we are brought into eternal life. Saint Paul believed in this so strongly that he looked forward to his death. He wrote: "For to me life is Christ, and death is gain. If I go on living in the flesh, that means fruitful labor for me. . . . I am caught between the two. I long to depart this life and be with Christ, [for] that is far better" (Philippians 1:21–23). ✝

Article 33 Heaven, Hell, and Purgatory

Most people would rather not think too much about their own death. It is not usually too hard to avoid thinking about, because early deaths are rare in the United States and most developed countries. Most young people can get all the way through high school and attend only a handful of funerals. Yet every once in a while, because of an accident or a serious illness or the death of someone close to us, we have to face the possibility of our own death. In these times the thought that races through most people's minds is, "What will happen to me when I die?"

Heaven

A state of eternal life and union with God in which one experiences full happiness and the satisfaction of the deepest human longings.

Christians already know the answer to that question. We have the advantage because the person who supplied the answers has actually died and risen from the dead! After death our soul will be judged and those that have remained faithful to God will be united with him in Heaven. Those who separated themselves from God in this life will be separated from him for all eternity in Hell. Believing in Jesus' promise that we will rise to new life does not completely take away the sting of death, but our faith does help us to understand that death is not an end but a new and glorious beginning.

Heaven

What exactly is **Heaven?** Neither the Bible nor the Tradition of the Church has a definitive description of Heaven. What we do know is that in Heaven the relationship between God and humanity that was broken by Original Sin will be restored. In Heaven we will know the joy of being in perfect communion with the Holy Trinity, the relationship that God has intended for us from the beginning of time. Think of a moment when you were with a group of good friends and you had just done something really great and exciting—maybe you just won an important game or just finished a retreat or a big service project. Everyone was content and joyful and excited. That experience is a little bit like what Heaven will be like, except in Heaven it won't be just a moment—it will last for all eternity.

Even though we generally refer to Heaven as being up and Hell as being down, they are not physical places as we experience time and space. Thus we can describe them through metaphors and analogies only. For example, when speaking of Heaven, Jesus uses the metaphor of a mansion: "In my Father's house there are many dwelling places. If there were not, would I have told you that I am going to prepare a place for you?" (John 14:2). Some of the most powerful descriptions of Heaven come from the Book of Revelation. Consider these examples:

> I heard a loud voice from the throne saying, "Behold, God's dwelling is with the human race. He will dwell with them and they will be his people and God himself will always be with them [as their God]. He will wipe every tear from their eyes, and there shall be no more death or mourning, wailing or pain, [for] the old order has passed away." (21:3–4)

The Martyrdom of Saint Ignatius of Antioch

Ignatius of Antioch is a Church Father who was born around AD 50 and was martyred around AD 100. He was bishop of Antioch when a terrible persecution of Christians broke out under the Roman emperor Domitian. He witnessed to the early Christians his joyful anticipation of Heaven. He himself was arrested and found guilty of treason. He was sent to Rome to be torn apart by wild beasts. Not only did Ignatius face this bravely, but, in his letter to the Romans, he begged them not to try to save him:

All the pleasures of the world, and all the kingdoms of this earth, shall profit me nothing. It is better for me to die in behalf of Jesus Christ, than to reign over all the ends of the earth. "For what shall a man be profited, if he gain the whole world, but lose his own soul?" Him I seek, who died for us: Him I desire, who rose again for our sake. This is the gain which is laid up for me. . . . Allow me to obtain pure light: when I have gone there, I shall indeed be a man of God. Permit me to be an imitator of the passion of my God.

Then the angel showed me the river of life-giving water, sparkling like crystal, flowing from the throne of God and of the Lamb down the middle of its street. On either side of the river grew the tree of life that produces fruit twelve times a year, once each month; the leaves of the trees serve as medicine for the nations. Nothing accursed will be found there any more. The throne of God and of the Lamb will be in it, and his servants will worship him. They will look upon his face, and his name will be on their foreheads. Night will be no more, nor will they need light from lamp or sun, for the Lord God shall give them light, and they shall reign forever and ever. (22:1–5)

The title of this image is "Heaven and Hell." How do you see this title reflected in the elements of the painting?

© Images.com/Corbis

Hell

Hell

The eternal punishment of separation from God, reserved for those who die in mortal sin and are unrepentant, thus freely and consciously rejecting God at the end of their lives.

Purgatory

A state of final purification or cleansing, which one may need to enter following death and before entering Heaven.

Hell will be the opposite of Heaven. It is the eternal punishment of separation from God, reserved for those who die in mortal sin without repenting and accepting God's merciful love. In describing the Final Judgment, Jesus says, "Depart from me, you accursed, into the eternal fire prepared for the devil and his angels" (Matthew 25:41). And the Book of Revelation says this: "Then Death and Hades were thrown into the pool of fire. (This pool of fire is the second death.) Anyone whose name was not found written in the book of life was thrown into the pool of fire" (20:14–15). Some scholars think the inspiration for describing Hell as a place of fire came from the garbage pit outside Jerusalem. The pit was often burning, filled with things that no longer filled their purpose.

Popular images of Hell are usually of burning pits and of demons with pitchforks torturing the unfortunate souls who end up there for eternity. Hell is indeed a reality. But the principal punishment isn't physical torture; it is the spiritual anguish of being separated from God. Think of Hell as the natural and logical consequence for a person who had already decided to separate herself or himself from God here on earth. Once on this journey, a person drifts further and further into sin and away from the One who is the source of all life and happiness. At death that separation becomes complete.

Purgatory

But the reality is that when most of us die, we are neither perfect saints nor perfect sinners. We believe in God and desire God's grace, yet areas of our lives may need to be purged of selfishness and sin. All who die in God's grace and friendship, but who are not perfectly purified undergo a purification in order to achieve the holiness necessary to enter fully into the glory of God in Heaven. This state of final purification is called **Purgatory.** Whether a soul is in need of Purgatory is something known to God

Catholics believe our prayers for the dead honor them and can aid in their final purification.

© Lisa F. Young/istockphoto.com

Pray It!

Prayer for the Deceased

Saint Cyril of Jerusalem said, "We pray . . . for all who have fallen asleep before us, in the belief that it is a great benefit to [their] souls." Quite often on the night before a funeral, a rite called the Vigil for the Deceased is held to pray for the person who has died. The opening prayer of this rite is a wonderful prayer that acknowledges our pain in losing a loved one and also celebrates the hope of eternal life:

Lord our God,
[Death reminds us of] our human condition
and the brevity of our lives on earth.
But for those who believe in your love
death is not the end,
nor does it destroy the bonds
that you forge in our lives.
We share the faith of your Son's disciples
and the hope of the children of God.
Bring the light of Christ's resurrection
to this time of testing and pain
as we pray for [the deceased] and for those who love him / her,
through Christ our Lord.
Amen.

(Order of Christian Funerals)

alone. Souls in Purgatory are assured of entering Heaven once their purification is complete. This belief is part of the truth God has revealed in Tradition and in Sacred Scripture. In Scripture we encounter references to the idea of purification after death in both the Old Testament and the New Testament. In 2 Maccabees we read of making atonement for the dead in order to free them from sin (12:46). In the New Testament, Saint Paul speaks of a person being saved through a purifying fire (see 1 Corinthians 3:15). ✝

Part Review

1. Describe four consequences of sin the Paschal Mystery saves us *from*.

2. How would you describe the meaning of death for those who die in God's grace?

3. Name four things the Paschal Mystery saves us *for*.

4. How do we already share in Christ's death and Resurrection?

5. Describe the difference between our particular judgment and the Final Judgment.

6. What is the Parousia?

7. What is the main difference between Heaven and Hell?

8. How would you describe Purgatory to someone who had never heard of it?

The Paschal Mystery and Your Life

Part 1

Living as a Disciple

The first three sections of this book describe God's plan of salvation, which culminates in the Paschal Mystery. Now we turn our attention to what the Paschal Mystery means for our lives. Through the Paschal Mystery, God calls us and strengthens us to be active participants in his plan. This means he calls us to become perfect in our love for him, our love for other people, and our love for all creation. In other words, we are called to be holy people.

Through our Baptism, God gives us the grace to live out our call to holiness. This requires effort on our part. We need to exercise spiritual and moral discipline because we are in a spiritual battle, fighting against our own conflicting inner desires and fighting against the pull of a world still affected by Satan's influence. As disciples of Jesus Christ, we turn to him for strength and guidance; he is the source of our salvation and our model for a holy life. We unite our lives to his life by following his example. In particular, we are called to participate in Christ's threefold ministry of priest, prophet, and king. In these articles we explore what this means for us today.

The topics covered in this part are:

- Article 34: "Our Call to Holiness" (page 151)

- Article 35: "Participating in Christ's Priestly Ministry" (page 155)

- Article 36: "Participating in Christ's Prophetic Ministry" (page 159)

- Article 37: "Participating in Christ's Kingly Ministry" (page 164)

Article 34 Our Call to Holiness

You are called to be holy. What do you think when you hear this? Does it seem like an impossible goal? Does it seem like something people expect of clergy and vowed religious only? Does it conjure up images of people who are at Church all the time, attending everything offered by your parish?

There is some truth in each of these. Being holy is a lifelong commitment and challenge, but it is not an impossible goal. Clergy and vowed religious should be examples of holiness, but so should every Christian. The Church does help us to live holy lives, but we are called to bring our holiness into the world, to help our families, our schools, and our workplaces become holy. Don't let any of these questions or doubts become an excuse for avoiding your own call to be a holy person.

What Is Holiness?

Holiness is difficult to describe because it has many dimensions and meanings. Let's consider three of these dimensions to help you understand your own call to be holy.

First, something is holy because it somehow reveals God and shares in God's own life. In a general sense, all creation is holy. But in a particular sense, every human being is holy in a special way. Each of us is made in God's own image and likeness, so we reveal God and are in communion with God in a way no other part of creation is. We are holy because we are made in the image of God.

Second, something is holy when it has been **consecrated** to God; that is, it has been solemnly designated or set aside for service to God. In the Gospel of John, at the Last Supper, Jesus says, "I consecrate myself for them, so that they also may be consecrated in truth" (17:19). Jesus completely dedicated himself to his Father's purpose. We are holy because we have been consecrated to God through our Baptism. Christ now lives in us, and we share in his holiness. In Baptism we too have been solemnly designated for service to God.

Third, in the Bible something is holy because it is considered "clean," free from anything that would make it impure. Thus the animals brought for sacrifice had to be healthy, strong, and without blemish or physical defects.

holiness

The state of being holy. This means to be set apart for God's service, to live a morally good life, to be a person of prayer, and to reveal God's love to the world through acts of loving service.

consecrate

To declare or set apart as sacred or to solemnly dedicate to God's service; to make holy.

Similarly, we must be morally clean, free from the impurity of sin. We are holy because we have clean hearts and clean consciences. We are not burdened with unrepented sin, and we do not give scandal to the Gospel of Jesus Christ by immoral behavior.

So what does it mean to be holy? We could summarize it like this: We are holy from the moment of our conception because we are made in the image and likeness of God. Our holiness is corrupted, however, because of Original Sin. Baptism restores our original holiness and consecrates us to God's service. As baptized people we perfect our holiness by avoiding sin and dedicating our lives to the service of others, following the example of Jesus.

Aids to Holiness

In the Sermon on the Mount, Jesus says at one point, "So be perfect, just as your heavenly Father is perfect" (Matthew 5:48). Jesus isn't talking about being a perfect athlete or a

Live It!

Daily Schedule for a Holy Teenager

6:30	Rise and say morning prayers
6:40	Shower, dress, and eat breakfast
7:45	Go to school
3:00	Attend extracurricular activities
5:00	Go home
6:00	Eat dinner
7:00	Do homework and chat online
10:30	Say night prayers and go to bed

Are you surprised by this schedule? Did you think there would be Church meetings and prayer groups? Being a holy person is not so much about *what* you do, but rather *how* you do it. Prayer is an essential element, but this does not mean you have to sit alone in a room to pray for hours. Short prayers before, during, and after meals and other activities are appropriate to a young person's daily life.

Besides prayer, living a holy life means many things: helping your friend to study for a test; choosing to be honest in school and in your relationships; being a hopeful person; feeding your body, mind, and soul with good things; standing up for the outcasts; and treating yourself and everyone around you as the children of God. Mother Teresa said it best: "You have to be holy where you are—wherever God has put you."

grace
The free and unde-
served gift of God's
loving and active
presence in our lives,
empowering us to
respond to his call and
to live as his adopted
sons and daughters.
Grace restores our lov-
ing communion with
the Holy Trinity, lost
through sin.

perfect student or a perfect musician of course. In the context of the Sermon on the Mount, it is clear that he is talking about being perfect in living a life of holiness. This is not an easy task. The *Catechism of the Catholic Church* says, "The way of perfection passes by the way of the Cross. There is no holiness without renunciation and spiritual battle"[1] (2015). Being holy means having to say no to things other people are saying yes to. And it will be a struggle.

We are not without help, however. God provides us with many things to guide us and strengthen us on our path to holiness. You have heard of these gifts, but it helps to be reminded of them.

Intellect and Free Will

Every human being is born with intellect and free will. Our intellect helps us to see and understand the natural order God has created. It helps us to weigh decisions and evaluate outcomes in order to make good moral choices. And our free will allows us to act on those good choices, sometimes even if no one else is.

Grace

Grace is God's supernatural gift to help us to respond to his love, to restore us to original holiness and justice, and to help us live holy lives. Through grace we participate in the life of the Holy Trinity with God as our Father, Jesus as our brother, and the Holy Spirit as the one who lives within us and gives us strength and guidance. Various kinds of grace assist us on our way to perfection.

Types of Grace

Grace is the free and undeserved help God gives us to respond to his call on our journey to holiness. Here are some of the different types of grace we can receive.

Type of Grace	Description
Sanctifying Grace	Through Baptism we receive sanctifying grace and a share in the divine life. This is a permanent disposition, a change in us that orients us toward God and helps us to live in keeping with his call. It heals our sins and restores our friendship with God.
Actual Grace	God's intervention and support for us in the everyday moments of our lives. Actual grace is important for our continuing growth in holiness.
Sacramental Grace	The gifts specific to each of the Seven Sacraments.
Special Grace	Also called "charisms," special grace is associated with one's state in life and is intended to build up the Body of Christ.

Self-Reflection

God has given us the ability, and the responsibility, to engage in self-reflection or **interiority.** This gift allows us to remove ourselves from the noise and distractions of everyday life. Then, in the silence of our hearts, we can look at the direction our life is heading, examine the choices we've made, and listen for and follow the voice of our conscience.

© Mika Heittola/Shutterstock.com

Taking time for self-reflection is an important tool for growing in holiness. When and where do you take time to reflect?

The Church

The Church is certainly God's greatest gift to us in living holy lives. The Church's sacramental life unites us to Christ and provides us with the gifts and guidance of the Holy Spirit. As the Body of Christ, the members of the Church give strength, hope, and support to one another in our common goal of becoming holy people. The Church provides us with opportunities for education, for prayer, for community, and for service to the world. Christ has given the Church the gift of holiness. As members of the Church, we share in that gift.

Answer God's call to become a holy person! Take time away from the rush and noise of the world to meet Jesus in the silence of your heart. Then go out into the world and let Christ's holiness shine through you to bring his love to others. God has forgiven you; now let his forgiveness touch the hearts of others through you. Let your positive moral choices influence others to make the right choices. Let acts of humble and loving service show others they are not alone; they are loved by God. "So be perfect, just as your heavenly Father is perfect." ✝

interiority

The practice of developing a life of self-reflection and self-examination to attend to your spiritual life and your call to holiness.

laity

All members of the Church with the exception of those who are ordained as bishops, priests, or deacons. The laity share in Christ's role as priest, prophet, and king, witnessing to God's love and power in the world.

Article 35 Participating in Christ's Priestly Ministry

In describing the role of the **laity** in the Church, the *Dogmatic Constitution on the Church* (*Lumen Gentium,* 1964), a Second Vatican Council document, uses the images of priest, prophet, and king. These titles, all biblical in origin, refer to offices that people are established in through anointing. These titles are given to Jesus Christ, the Anointed One, to describe his saving work in the world. But the bishops of the world teach us that because we are called to participate in Christ's mission through our Baptism, these titles describe our Christian identity too. The *Catechism of the Catholic Church* says: "Jesus Christ is the one whom the Father anointed with the Holy Spirit and established as priest, prophet, and king. The whole People of God participates in these three offices of Christ and bears the responsibilities for the mission and service that flow from them"[2] (783).

You might say: "I'm not a priest, a prophet, or a king. How can these roles apply to me?" This is a very good question. We are familiar with the role of priest, but prophet and king are not roles we hear about too often in our time. So let's take a closer look at each of these titles in this and the next two articles.

© Burstein Collection/CORBIS

Christ's Priestly Ministry

At the time Jesus was on earth, a Jewish priest had one primary role—to lead the worship in the Temple. This primarily meant offering animal sacrifice. The priests were divided into twenty-four divisions, and each division worked in the Temple one week out of every twenty-four. When they were not on duty in the Temple, priests served as judges, teachers of the Torah (the Scriptures), and scribes (copying texts or writing up legal documents).

As our high priest, Jesus' sacrifice makes possible our salvation. How do you participate in his priestly ministry?

Catholic Wisdom

The Priesthood of the Laity

This excerpt from *Dogmatic Constitution on the Church* (*Lumen Gentium,* 1964) shows how the bishops of the Second Vatican Council called on the laity to fully live out their priestly mission:

All the disciples of Christ, persevering in prayer and praising God, should present themselves as a living sacrifice, holy and pleasing to God. . . . They live in the ordinary circumstances of family and social life. . . . They are called there by God that . . . they may work for the sanctification of the world from within . . . [and] make Christ known to others, especially by the testimony of a life resplendent in faith, hope and charity. (10 and 31)

By now you know that Jesus was not a priest in this sense. As far as we know, he never offered animal sacrifice in the Temple. Yet the author of the Letter to the Hebrews repeatedly calls Jesus a high priest. He says this because Jesus perfectly fulfilled the sacrificial role of the Jewish priests. The Jewish priests offered animal sacrifice for the forgiveness of the people's sins, but this sacrifice had to be repeated. Jesus offered a single sacrifice for the forgiveness of all sin, and this sacrifice was sufficient for all people for all time. His sacrifice was his own body and blood. So Jesus, our great high priest, teaches us how to pray, worship, and sacrifice.

Jesus has a lot to teach us about prayer. Jesus was committed to personal prayer, often rising early in the morning to pray alone (see Mark 1:35). He was also committed to communal prayer, joining others in local synagogues on the Sabbath to read the Scriptures and pray together (see Luke 4:16). His prayer included praise and thanksgiving (see 10:21) and prayers of petition and supplication (see John, chapter 17). (These prayer forms are explained in the article "Why We Pray," on page 184.) Jesus taught us that our prayer should be humble and honest (see Luke 18:10–14); it is not too strong to say that Jesus despised prayer that was showy and hypocritical.

Jesus also taught us how to sacrifice. This will be covered more completely in the part titled "Suffering and the Paschal Mystery." For now, simply remember how Jesus dedicated his life for the good of others and called his disciples to do the same. In doing this he sacrificed human comforts and luxuries: "Foxes have dens and birds of the sky have nests, but the Son of Man has nowhere to rest his head" (Matthew 8:20). He made it clear that he expected his disciples to do the same: "Whoever wishes to come after me must deny himself, take up his cross, and follow me" (16:24).

How You Can Participate

Because we have been united to Christ through Baptism and Confirmation, all laypeople share in Christ's priesthood. God calls us to exhibit the graces we receive in the Sacraments in all the dimensions of our lives, with our family, with our school and work, with our church family, with our community and nation. In doing this we fulfill our call to holiness. Perhaps ideas on how you can participate in Christ's priestly ministry are already coming to you. Here are some foundations for making his priestly ministry an integral part of your life:

- **Take time to pray daily.** This doesn't have to be a long time or even heavily structured. But take a few minutes of private, quiet time to recognize the presence of God and ask his help to make the day a holy day. You could read a few verses of Scripture, read a short spiritual reflection, or say a prayer that focuses your mind and heart on your call to be a disciple.
- **Attend Mass every week.** Jesus attended the synagogue every Sabbath because reflecting on the Scriptures and worshipping his Father with other faithful believers is important for strengthening faith. The same is even truer for us. At every Eucharist we receive Christ through his Word and through his sacred Body and Blood. This is not just a nice thing to do; it is central to our faith because the Eucharist is the foundation

Saint Benedict the Moor

Benedict Manasseri was the child of Ethiopian parents who were taken as slaves to Italy in the early 1500s. His parents converted to Christianity before his birth. Benedict worked from childhood alongside his family for meager wages, showing his willingness to sacrifice by giving what he had earned to those with greater needs and to the sick. He never learned to read and write.

When Benedict was twenty-one years old, he was publicly insulted because of his color. Some Franciscans noticed this and invited him to join their order. Benedict agreed and showed his devotion to a private life of prayer by becoming a **hermit.** But God had other things in store for him. Benedict was asked to join a Franciscan community where he started as cook and ended up being the community superior, despite the fact that he was illiterate and a lay brother. Benedict is a wonderful example of a person's fully participating in the priestly ministry of Christ. His feast day is April 4, and he is the patron saint of African Americans.

of Christian life. Attending Sunday Eucharist, a precept of the Church and required by the Third Commandment, is such an important obligation that if we don't attend through our own fault, we commit mortal sin and must receive absolution in the Sacrament of Penance and Reconciliation before receiving Communion again.

- **Participate regularly in the Sacrament of Penance and Reconciliation**. The importance of regular participation in the Eucharist was just discussed. It is just as important to celebrate the one other Sacrament that we are called to participate in regularly throughout our lives: Penance and Reconciliation. Through our repentance and God's forgiveness of our sins, we grow in holiness and prevent sin from leading us away from God.

- **Sacrifice time and comfort to share God's love.** For many people this is not an easy thing to do. We live in a culture that in many ways tells us we deserve whatever we want, whenever we want. But that attitude will not ultimately make us happy or holy people. When we make sacrifices to help others, whether those sacrifices be our time, our money, or our comforts, we will know the true peace and joy that comes from uniting ourselves with Jesus Christ.

You may be able to think of many other ways to participate in the priestly ministry of Christ. Devote yourself to becoming a person of prayer and sacrifice, and your holiness will grow, day by day. ✝

hermit
A person who lives a solitary life in order to commit himself or herself more fully to prayer and in some cases to be completely free for service to others.

Article 36 Participating in Christ's Prophetic Ministry

Do you know someone who likes to speak out for important causes, someone who encourages other people to do the right thing? Maybe you know someone who is committed to a justice concern like ending abortion or providing affordable housing for all people. Maybe you have seen people who share with others their faith in Jesus. Maybe you are a person like this.

Christians who do these things are participating in the prophetic ministry of Christ. As prophets we witness to Christ through our words and actions, we witness to every group and in every circumstance in which we find ourselves. As laypeople we witness in places where clergy are often not found: work, politics, sports, and so on. This is also called evangelization, a word that literally means "to announce good news." By calling for greater love and justice in the world, we are sharing God's desire that all people know his love and justice.

Christ's Prophetic Ministry

Jesus perfectly fulfilled the role of prophet. A prophet gives voice to God's Word, proclaiming it to those who need to hear it. Because Jesus is God, his every word and action proclaim the divine Word to the world. In the Gospel of John, Jesus is very clear that his words and actions have revealed his Father: "If you know me, then you will also know my Father. . . . Whoever has seen me has seen the Father" (14:7,9). Ultimately, Jesus' prophetic ministry had one primary focus: to lead people to the one, true God.

Given that all of Jesus' words and actions are prophetic, it is difficult or maybe even misleading to identify the fulfill-

Pray It!

Fellow Prophets, Pray for Us

As Christians we are all called to be prophets. It can be a difficult job (see Matthew 5:12) and cannot be done without relying on God's help. We can get some guidance by looking to the example and the support of the prophets who have gone before us. Let us call on them to pray for us.

Lord,

We need your help. As we go into the world to care for those who are oppressed and needy, to speak out against injustice, and to proclaim the Good News, grant us the gifts of the prophets before us.

Give us courage. Oscar Romero, pray for us.

Give us humility. Blessed Teresa of Calcutta, pray for us.

Give us strength. Saint Thomas More, pray for us.

Give us trust. Jeremiah, pray for us.

Give us goodness. Blessed John XXIII, pray for us.

Give us concern for the poor. Dorothy Day, pray for us.

Give us selflessness. Saint Maximillian Kolbe, pray for us.

All you holy people, pray for us!

Amen.

ment of his prophetic ministry with a particular teaching or action. However, we can see how his words and actions were in the tradition of the prophets of the Old Testament. Here is a chart of some of those parallels:

Old Testament Prophetic Themes	Parallels in Jesus' Words and Actions
The prophets called the people to reject idolatry, the worship of false gods (for example Isaiah 10:10-11; Jeremiah 32:34-35; Hosea 13:2).	Jesus called for an end to the worship of money and possessions, a form of idolatry (for example Matthew 6:19-24; Luke 12:13-34)..
The prophets called for the care of the most vulnerable in society, particularly the widow, the orphan, and the stranger (for example Isaiah 1:17; Jeremiah 7:6; Zechariah 7:10).	Jesus healed the most vulnerable people of his time. He said that in the Final Judgment, we would be judged by our service to the most vulnerable people (Matthew 25:31-46).
The prophets called for an end to societal injustice. They called for the powerful to protect the poor and vulnerable (for example, Micah 3:1-4; Amos 2:6-8).	Jesus called on the wealthy to practice justice by sharing their wealth with those in need (Luke 12:33; 14:7-14; 16:19-31). He said true leaders were the servants of others (Mark 10:43-44).
The prophets called for an end to hypocritical worship of God (for example, Isaiah 1:11-15; Jeremiah 6:20). They called people to worship God with a pure heart.	Jesus disrupted the moneychangers and the sale of sacrificial animals in the Temple, a hypocritical practice (Matthew 21:12-13). He called for authentic worship (John 4:23-24).

Keep in mind that although Jesus followed in the tradition of the Old Testament prophets, he is not just a prophet.

How You Can Participate

The world needs the prophetic ministry of Christ in many ways. Be open to whatever way God is calling you to be a prophet. There are big things and small things you can do, and all of them are important. Here are some things young people have already done:

- **Speak out for the unborn.** Join the fight against abortion by letting others know that abortion, the murder of an unborn child, is a sin against God's Law, and that it also causes emotional and spiritual harm to the mother and those connected to her unborn child, especially her other children and the father of the child. Write to

Saint Martin de Porres

Martin de Porres was born in 1579 in Lima, Peru, the illegitimate son of a Spanish nobleman and a freed black slave. He grew up in poverty, and at age fifteen he joined the Dominican friary as a servant. Although the friary had a rule against blacks becoming full members, they dropped the rule when they saw Martin's great piety. He eventually became a full brother and was placed in charge of the infirmary.

Martin had a great commitment to the poor and to justice for slaves. He established an orphanage and a children's hospital for the poor. He collected alms, which he used to feed hundreds of poor people regularly. Miraculous cures were attributed to him; he sometimes brought healing with just a cup of water. When an epidemic struck the city, Martin tirelessly cared for those taken ill, risking his own life and health. Martin de Porres is an inspirational example of full participation in the prophetic ministry of Christ. His feast day is November 3. He is the patron saint of people of mixed race and also the patron saint of social justice.

your legislators asking them to vote to limit and end abortions and to work to reduce the poverty that makes some pregnant women feel abortion is their only option. Collect baby items and hold fundraisers for groups that help to support pregnant women who are in need.

- **Speak out against violence in your community.** Jesus warned us against the evil of violence and revenge. Teens have organized campaigns against bullying and other violence in their schools, communities, and social groups. Violence flourishes when people ignore it or turn the other way. Make sure the leaders in your

community know about the presence of violence in families, schools, or neighborhoods.

- **Organize to help people in need.** Jesus spent much of his time helping the people in his community with the greatest needs. Young people have helped others to experience God's love by organizing food drives, clothing drives, hunger walks, Christmas collections, and many, many other needs. You can volunteer to help build homes for people who need them or to clean up after a natural disaster. You don't have to be rich or skilled in some trade; you just have to be willing and committed to helping in whatever way you can.

- **Share your love of God with others.** There are many people in our world who need to hear that God loves them. Young people have shared the love of God by becoming **catechists** of younger children and volunteering on retreat teams and mission trips. You can join online social networks to talk about God with others. You can watch for friends and classmates who are troubled or hurting and offer a kind heart and a listening ear.

These are only some of the many ways you can participate in the prophetic ministry of Christ. Pray for the courage and commitment to live your faith publicly and for the willingness to share your faith with others. ✞

catechesis, catechists

Catechesis is the process by which Christians of all ages are taught the essentials of Christian doctrine and are formed as disciples of Christ. Catechists instruct others in Christian doctrine and for entry into the Church.

By organizing and participating in works of service, we share in Christ's prophetic and kingly ministry. How do you serve others?

© Ariel Skelley/Blend Images/Corbis

Article 37 Participating in Christ's Kingly Ministry

That man is rightly called a king who makes his own body an obedient subject and, by governing himself with suitable rigor, refuses to let his passions breed rebellion in his soul, for he exercises a kind of royal power over himself.

—Saint Ambrose

Only one who devotes himself to a cause with his whole strength and soul can be a true master. For this reason mastery demands all of a person.

—Albert Einstein

If a king is zealous for the rights of the poor,
    his throne stands firm forever.

—Proverbs 29:14

You have royal blood in you, for you are an adopted son or daughter of God. What does it mean to be "kingly," to be a leader from God's point of view? The quotations above suggest that it starts with self-discipline, to consistently choose what is good and right. It continues with our commitment to follow God's call with all our strength and soul for our entire life. And it means always serving those most in need.

Christ's Kingly Ministry

Christ's kingly ministry is unlike most earthly versions of kings and rulers that come to mind. To understand his kingship, we need to clear our mind of images of kings and leaders who seek their own fame or their own gain. In answer to Pilate's question, "Are you the king of the Jews?" Jesus answers in part, "My kingdom does not belong to this world" (John 18:33,36). Jesus does not deny that he is a king, but he will not allow Pilate or any earthly authority to define what his kingship means.

In an earlier article, we established that the Kingdom of God is the fulfillment of the promise or covenant God made with David, "Your house and your kingdom shall endure forever before me; your throne shall stand firm forever" (2 Samuel 7:16). Jesus Christ is the King of Kings whose Kingdom will last forever. We have to carefully research Jesus' words and actions in the New Testament, though, to understand what his kingship truly is. Three key passages will help to make this clearer.

The first passage is Jesus' temptation in the desert at the beginning of his ministry. In the second temptation, the Devil shows Jesus all the kingdoms of the world and promises to make him the ruler of all of them if Jesus would only worship the Devil. Jesus quotes Deuteronomy 6:13 in his response: "You shall worship the Lord, your God, / and him alone shall you serve" (Luke 4:8). Jesus refuses to become a ruler through any compromise with evil. Jesus' leadership is completely rooted in obedience and service to God. It is a leadership that is completely committed to doing the right thing. Jesus knows that a good end can never be achieved through sinful means. Even when his commitment to doing the right thing results in personal suffering and seeming failure, Jesus never veers from the holy and moral path.

The second passage is when two of Jesus' Apostles ask if they can sit in places of honor, at his left side and his right side, when he comes into his glory. This request understandably upset the other Apostles. Jesus uses this as a teaching moment: "You know that those who are recognized as rulers over the Gentiles lord it over them, and their great ones make their authority over them felt. But it shall not be so among you. Rather, whoever wishes to be great among you will be your servant; whoever wishes to be first among you will be the slave of all" (Mark 10:42–44). Jesus refers to the Romans' use of power and entitlement in order to maintain control over the population. Jesus is clear that this is not true leadership. In the Kingdom of God, those who lead are first the servants of others. Jesus leads by his example of love and concern for others.

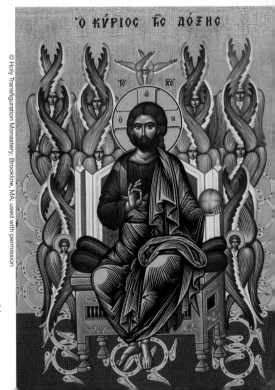

The third passage is a parable Jesus told in which a king or a prominent man throws a banquet but the invited guests refuse to attend.

Saint Katharine Drexel

Katharine Drexel was born in 1858 in Philadelphia, the daughter of a wealthy Philadelphia banker. As a young woman, she was moved by the needs of African Americans and Native Americans. She used her family's wealth to build schools for their education. She visited Pope Leo XIII to ask for missionaries to staff her schools. He suggested that she become a missionary herself. So in 1891 she founded the Sisters of the Blessed Sacrament for Indians and Colored People and became the order's first mother superior.

From the age of thirty-three until her death at age ninety-six (March 3, 1955), Katharine dedicated her personal wealth to her ministry. She herself lived a life of voluntary poverty, wearing the same pair of shoes every day for ten years. Her crowning achievement was the building of Xavier University in 1915, the first college for African Americans in the country. At the time of her death, more than five hundred sisters were teaching in sixty-three schools. Mother Drexel was canonized by Pope John Paul II in 2000, only the second recognized American-born saint. Her feast day is March 3.

© Bettmann/CORBIS

And so the king tells his servants, "Go out, therefore, into the main roads and invite to the feast whomever you find" (Matthew 22:9). In Luke he says, "Go out quickly into the streets and alleys of the town and bring in here the poor and the crippled, the blind and the lame" (14:21). Jesus is teaching that leaders in the Kingdom of God will not be focused on people who can return favors; rather, leaders in the Kingdom of God will reach out to all people, especially the people whom worldly leaders overlook.

This is Jesus' example of kingly ministry. It is leadership that is based in a moral life committed to personal holiness. It is leadership that does not focus on our own fame or gain; rather, it focuses on being of service to others. It is leadership that reaches out to all people, especially the people overlooked by polite society. You are called to share in Jesus' kingly ministry, to be this kind of leader for the Kingdom of God.

How You Can Participate

You may have noticed that the characteristics of Jesus Christ's threefold ministry of priest, prophet, and king overlap to some degree. These three ministerial roles do not have sharp distinctions. They are three ways of describing the same reality: what it means to be a disciple of Christ. So some of the ways already mentioned for participating in Christ's priestly and prophetic ministry can also be ways for participating in his kingly ministry. The important focus in Christ's kingly ministry is the attitude we bring to our words and actions.

- **Be outstanding in your personal morality.** You must be committed to living a morally pure life. Avoid sin and temptation. Participate frequently in the Eucharist and in the Sacrament of Penance and Reconciliation to strengthen yourself with God's graces. Do not succumb to the temptation to try to achieve a good result if it means lying, cheating, intentionally hurting someone, denying your faith, or taking any other moral shortcut.

- **Find work or service that in some way helps others.** Make a commitment to make a difference in the world. Ask God to lead you to wherever you are needed—and then be ready to go there. It may take some time to find a service that really fits, so be willing to try different things.

- **Be humble.** Being a holy leader will have its own spiritual rewards, but these will not come if your primary reason for volunteering your service is to call attention to yourself or to seek some kind of personal gain. Always examine your motives as a leader. Be humble and acknowledge that your gifts for leadership and service come from God and are to be used for the good of others.

- **Have a servant attitude.** Let your first thought be, "How can I help?" Don't get caught up in wanting to do only the "important" tasks. Remember that Jesus washed the feet of his disciples to show that no act of service is unimportant. A holy leader does whatever is needed to help build the Kingdom of God.

Each Christian is called to participate in Christ's kingship in some way, to be a holy leader. Our world desperately needs such leaders, but it is not an easy path to take. Often the world models leadership that is built on moral compromise or on personal ego or on financial gain. Frequently ask the Holy Spirit to strengthen you and guide you in being a servant leader in your home, school, and community. ✝

Part Review

1. What are three ways that can be used to describe what it means to be holy?

2. What is one aid to holiness that God has given us? Describe how this aid helps us to be holy.

3. How can we say that Jesus Christ has a priestly ministry when he never was a Jewish priest?

4. What are two ways you can participate in Christ's priestly ministry?

5. How does Jesus' prophetic ministry follow the tradition of the Old Testament prophets?

6. What are two ways you can participate in Christ's prophetic ministry?

7. What are some of the characteristics of Jesus' kingly ministry?

8. What are two ways you can participate in Christ's kingly ministry?

Part 2

Suffering and the Paschal Mystery

Suffering is an essential part of the Paschal Mystery; recall that we describe the Paschal Mystery as the Passion (suffering), death, Resurrection, and Ascension of Jesus Christ. In fact, suffering is the first stage of the Paschal Mystery, a reality we often do not want to face. But suffering cannot be escaped; it is an inevitable part of being human. We experience both physical pain and emotional pain. We even experience spiritual suffering, the pain of separation from full communion with God.

Throughout history Christians have participated in the Paschal Mystery by accepting suffering and sacrifice as inevitable parts of life and as necessary consequences that come with following Christ. But there is good news. The Gospel proclaims that suffering is not our ultimate end. It is only a step on our path toward Heaven and eternal life. Even more, when we join our suffering to Christ's suffering, we are participating in God's saving work. These articles introduce this spiritual reality that you will encounter again and again throughout your life.

The topics covered in this part are:

Article 38 Making Sense of Suffering

We want life to make sense and to be fair, which is why we sometimes struggle with the reality of suffering. It does not seem rational to us that God—who is all good—would allow suffering to exist. Furthermore it seems very unfair that "good" people are just as prone to suffering as "bad" people. The Book of Job is essentially a debate over this very issue. Job was a good man but had some bad things happen to him. His friends thought Job must have been guilty of some kind of sin and kept arguing with Job that things would get better if he would just admit his sin. But Job maintained his innocence and demanded an audience with God to plead his case.

After many chapters Job gets his wish. God appears before him and proceeds to overwhelm him with questions about the mysteries of the universe that no human being could answer. At the end Job responds to God: "I know that you can do all things, / and that no purpose of yours is hindered. / I have dealt with great things that I do not understand; / things too wonderful for me, which I cannot know" (42:2–3). Job's response indicates that as human beings we are limited in what we can know and understand in God's great plan of salvation. Suffering is a mystery we cannot fully understand simply because we do not see things from God's perspective. This does not mean that it is completely incomprehensible. When we apply what we know about the history of salvation and the Paschal Mystery, we can begin to comprehend a part of this great mystery.

Where do you see suffering in the world today? In the story of Job, we learn that suffering is a mystery we cannot fully understand because we do not see things from God's perspective.

© Musee Bonnat, Bayonne, France/ Lauros/Giraudon/The Bridgeman Art Library International

Keys to Understanding

One key to understanding suffering is that it is due to Original Sin. After Adam and Eve's Fall, things that would not have caused human beings pain and suffering—symbolized by the consequences of pain during childbirth and the hard labor required to raise food (see Genesis 3:16–19)—now do cause pain and suffering. It was not a part of God's original plan for us. To save us from meaningless suffering and death, the Father sent his only begotten Son into the world. By assuming a human nature, Jesus made our suffering his own: "He took away our infirmities / and bore our diseases" (Matthew 8:17).

Another key to understanding suffering is that suffering and sacrifice are the pathway to redemption and salvation. Sacrifice is simply suffering that is freely accepted. You may have heard the saying "No pain, no gain." This reflects a deep spiritual truth. God can and will transform suffering and sacrifice into healing and new life. The animal sacrifices of

Pray It!

Trust In God

We must have one thing to make it through times of suffering: trust in God. Like Job, when we are lost and in the shadow of death, we must place our trust in God, knowing that he is with us in our pain and confusion.

Dear heavenly Father,
Life has been challenging for me lately.
The path before me is dark and uncertain.
I feel alone, even though I have people who care for me.
I feel anxious and afraid, even though Jesus tells us not to be.
I feel like I'm walking "through a dark valley" (Psalm 23:4)
    that has no end.

But I choose to place my trust in you,
believing that you love me and want the best for me.
I will trust you to guide me in the right path
even though I'm not sure right now what it is.
I will trust that you are with me
even though I do not feel your presence at this moment.
And I will trust that this dark time will pass
because you have given us the promise of eternal life.

the Chosen People recognized this spiritual truth. But those sacrifices were imperfect and insufficient. It is only through Christ's perfect sacrifice that death was destroyed and the doors to Heaven were opened, restoring the possibility of our full communion with God for all eternity.

Following Christ's example we too must accept suffering and make sacrifices as we work out our salvation. Jesus himself tells us that we need to do this: "You will be hated by all because of my name, but whoever endures until the end will be saved" and "Whoever does not take up his cross and follow after me is not worthy of me" (Matthew 10:22,38; highly recommended that you read all of chapter 10). Uniting our personal sufferings and sacrifices with Christ's is part of our priestly ministry. We do this not only because of our hope and faith in our eternal reward in Heaven but also to make up in some small way for the hurt and harm caused by our own personal sins.

Practical Examples of Sacrifice

Perhaps you might be saying, "I don't understand when and where I would possibly accept suffering as part of my life as a disciple." Consider these practical examples of sacrifice:

- when you choose to spend time with a sick classmate or family member instead of a fun afternoon or evening with friends
- when you choose to sacrifice personal popularity if it means participating in immoral activities
- when you prayerfully connect your experiences of illness and pain with the sufferings of Christ and accept them without becoming bitter and resentful
- when you willingly donate money and time to people in need instead of spending it on yourself
- when you make the sacrifice of time and comfort to use less energy, conserve and recycle natural resources, and protect the environment
- when you make your faith known publicly even if it leads to ridicule and sarcastic comments, or worse
- when you make the choice to remain a virgin until you are married even if it means sacrificing pleasure and relationships

It might seem that such sacrifices are impossible, that no one could do all these things. But Christians are making these sacrifices every day and accepting the suffering that comes with them. Not only have they discovered that the Holy Spirit provides the strength they need, but they have also discovered that paradoxically their lives are more meaningful and more joyful than before. ✞

Suffering in the Bible

The question of suffering is a theme that runs throughout the books of the Bible. Here is a weeklong study plan highlighting seven biblical passages that address this topic:

Day	Passage	Theme
1	Job, chapters 1, 6, 11, 40, 42	The Book of Job is a long debate about why we suffer. The chapters selected will give you a taste of the argument.
2	2 Maccabees 6:18–31	A Jewish martyr who accepts death from torture rather than deny his faith.
3	Isaiah 52:13—53:12	The Suffering Servant gives his life as an offering for sin.
4	Matthew, chapter 10	Jesus warns his disciples that they will be persecuted and have to sacrifice if they follow him.
5	John 15:18—16:15	Jesus promises his disciples that even though they will be persecuted, he is sending the Holy Spirit to guide and strengthen them.
6	2 Corinthians 1:3–11	Paul shares his conviction that God is with us and encourages us in our afflictions and sufferings.
7	1 Peter 3:13—4:6	Be willing to suffer for what is right just as Christ suffered.

Article 39 Is Accepting Suffering a Sign of Weakness?

It goes without saying that the most common reaction to suffering is to avoid it. In fact, many people would consider the willingness to sacrifice time, money, and worldly success foolish, a sign of personal weakness. This isn't a new phenomenon; even the early Christians struggled with this. In his First Letter to the Corinthians, Paul addresses the accusation that Christians are foolish to believe that salvation comes through Christ's suffering on the cross:

> The message of the cross is foolishness to those who are perishing, but to us who are being saved it is the power of God. . . . For the foolishness of God is wiser than human wisdom, and the weakness of God is stronger than human strength. . . . God chose the lowly and despised of this world, those who count for nothing, to reduce to nothing those who are something. (1 Corinthians 1:18,25,28)

The Example of Jesus

The example of Jesus clearly shows that the willingness to accept suffering takes a great deal of courage and strength. We see this clearly in Jesus' last days. He could have avoided his torturous death if he had wished to. He prayed to his Father that he might avoid this suffering if possible. Yet in the end, he accepted the necessity of accepting his Father's will with courage and strength. All four Gospels testify to this.

Catholic Wisdom

"True Love Causes Pain"

Few people have done more to ease the suffering of others than Blessed Teresa of Calcutta, or Mother Teresa. Here is some of her wisdom:

> We have to love until it hurts. It is not enough to say "I love." We must put that love into a living action. And how do we do that? By giving until it hurts. . . . True love causes pain. Jesus, in order to give us the proof of his love, died on a cross. A mother, in order to give birth to her baby, has to suffer. If you really love one another, you will not be able to avoid making sacrifices.

(*Mother Teresa: Her Essential Wisdom*)

Jesus' Passion and death are not the only times he demonstrates the strength and courage required for sacrificial love. He teaches it in his parables about the prodigal son and the lost sheep. He teaches it in his sayings about forgiveness and love of enemies. He demonstrates it by embracing a life of poverty and simplicity. He asks others to exercise moral courage by challenging wealthy and powerful people to give away their wealth and serve those in need.

Deep down every human heart knows that it is only through courage and sacrifice that we can truly achieve something worthwhile. But there is one more thing to add. **We must sacrifice for the right thing—to build the Kingdom of God.** Some people make tremendous sacrifices to achieve personal fame and fortune. And when they have achieved their success, they are still left feeling that they are missing something. They are missing the love and joy that come from letting Christ live in our heart, from joining our life to his life, from participating in his mission to bring God's love to others. This is a sacrifice that people simply cannot understand without God's help—it seems foolish. This is why we have to act as God's hands and voice, to show them and teach them the wisdom of the cross. ✝

© Brooklyn Museum/Corbis

Read the Parable of the Prodigal Son (Luke 15:11–32). How is the forgiving Father in this parable a sign of sacrificial love?

Saint Damien de Veuster

Fr. Damien de Veuster is better known as Damien of Molokai, the "apostle to the lepers." Damien's life is living proof that the willingness to endure suffering for the sake of following Christ is not a sign of weakness. Born in 1840 in Belgium, he became a missionary priest who ministered in the Hawaiian Islands. He later volunteered to minister to the leper colony on the island of Molokai, an assignment no one wanted for fear of contracting the disease. When Father Damien arrived, the colony was a wretched place. He acted as pastor, counselor, builder, and undertaker. Conditions in the colony improved immensely.

After twelve years on the island, Damien was diagnosed with **leprosy.** At first he was upset, wondering why God had not protected him from the disease. He worried about who would continue his work after his death. But he soon accepted his condition, describing himself as the "happiest missionary in the world." Help poured in from around the world and four new missionaries arrived at the island. Damien died in 1889 and was canonized on October 11, 2009, by Pope Benedict XVI. He is the patron saint of lepers and people with HIV / AIDS.

40 Finding Strength in Times of Suffering

leprosy
An infectious disease resulting in numbness, paralysis, and physical deformities; also called Hansen's disease. Effective treatment was not developed until the late 1930s.

Knowing that sacrifice and suffering have an important role in God's plan of salvation does not automatically make it easier to accept and endure suffering in our lives. To go from knowing this truth to living this truth is a spiritual journey we all must make. You may know from personal experience that this journey is not an easy one. You are even right to ask, "How can any person be expected to willingly sacrifice his or her own comfort and safety, even if it is for a greater good?"

The answer is that such sacrifice is impossible for us acting on our own. We can only do it by being empowered by our loving and compassionate God who desires to help us on that journey. This article looks at some key spiritual truths that have encouraged and strengthened Christians through the centuries in their journey to accept the sacrifices necessary for the Kingdom of God and unite their sufferings with the suffering of Christ.

Keys to Hope and Strength

First, and perhaps most important, we have the gift of knowing that we do not suffer alone. For some people the anguish caused by pain and suffering is multiplied by the feeling that they are alone in their pain. But Christians have the comfort of knowing that God is with us in our suffering. He is not aloof or removed from our suffering; our God and Savior suffered greatly in his Passion. And he has promised to be with us in everything we experience. In his final speech in the Gospel of John, Jesus gives us these words of comfort: "I will not leave you orphans; I will come to you. In a little while the world will no longer see me, but you will see me, because I live and you will live. On that day you will realize that I am in my Father and you are in me and I in you" (14:18–20). And later he continues: "As the Father loves me, so I also love you. Remain in my love. If you keep my commandments, you will remain in my love, just as I have kept my Father's commandments and remain in his love" (15:9–10).

fortitude

Also called strength or courage, the virtue that enables one to maintain sound moral judgment and behavior in the face of difficulties and challenges; one of the four cardinal virtues.

virtue

A habitual and firm disposition to do good.

One of the primary ways we experience God's caring presence is through the Church. In his famous analogy of the Body of Christ, Paul says, "If [one] part suffers, all the parts suffer with it" (1 Corinthians 12:26). Christians come to one another's aid in times of suffering. We spend time with the sick, we support the brokenhearted, we help those who have experienced disaster, we provide for those who are going through financial difficulties. This does not mean that everything will be made right or that your hardship will just disappear, but if you are part of an active faith community, you will find people to support you. Just be sure to make your needs known.

The gift of **fortitude,** or courage, is a second key to finding hope and strength in times of suffering. Fortitude is one of the Seven Gifts of the Holy Spirit that we receive through Baptism and that is strengthened at our Confirmation. You have only to ask for it when you need it, so ask often. Even the great Saint Paul speaks about his need for courage: "After we had suffered and been insolently treated, as you know, in Philippi, we drew courage through our God to speak to you the gospel of God with much struggle" (1 Thessalonians 2:2).

Fortitude is also a human **virtue** we must cultivate in our lives. It is one of the four cardinal virtues—prudence, justice, fortitude, and temperance—that are pivotal or essential for full Christian living. These virtues guide our actions in accordance with reason and faith so that we become persons

Live It!

Suffering Binds Us Together

In September of 2008, Hurricane Ike devastated Houston, Texas. Many houses were damaged or even totally destroyed. People lost electricity for weeks. But an amazing thing happened. Without television and air conditioning, neighbors came out of their homes and got to know one another. They helped one another by sharing chain saws, generators, ice coolers, and so on.

We often strive to be strong and independent (and in some ways that is good), but think about it—if you were totally self-sufficient, why would you need anyone? When we suffer, God wants us to support one another, not to suffer in silence. One of the worst things we can do is to suffer alone in silence. Not only does asking for other people's support help us, but it allows those people to live out their Christian mission. Suffering calls for us to ask for other people's help and support, binding us together as the Body of Christ and making us whole.

of moral character. They help us to control our passions so that we don't act impulsively or react immorally. So even though courage is a gift, it is also a virtue that grows through education, deliberate choices, and perseverance. God's grace will then purify and strengthen our courage. In this way courage becomes more and more a natural response when we are faced with fearful and painful situations.

A final key is in knowing that suffering is not the end of the story. We know how the Paschal Mystery ends, with Christ's Resurrection and Ascension into Heaven. The Paschal Mystery is God's promise that we too will experience resurrection and eternal life with God in Heaven if we are faithful in following Christ. We must look beyond our suffering to the joy and peace of Heaven, which will be ours for all eternity.

This is not to minimize the sacrifice and suffering many people experience. In fact, we have a responsibility to help wherever and however we can to diminish and eliminate suffering. Much suffering is the result of human violence and injustice, and we must challenge these sins just as Jesus did. But just as he did not eliminate suffering, neither can we hope to eliminate it. We accept that suffering is a part of every human life and that sacrifice is a part of every Christian's life, trusting that in the end God will make all things right. This is the promise of the Paschal Mystery, a promise you can bet your life on. ✝

Trust God is with you

Keys to Hope and Strength

Suffering is not the end of the story

Ask for fortitude

Saint Kateri Tekakwitha

Kateri Tekakwitha was born in present-day Auriesville, New York, in 1656, to a Christian Algonquin mother and a non-Christian Mohawk chief. When she was four, smallpox killed her parents and left her disfigured and partially blind. In later childhood, Kateri met Jesuit missionaries, and through their influence was baptized into the Church in 1676.

Kateri's new life made it difficult for her to remain in her village, as the other members of her tribe resented her new way of life as a follower of Christ and subjected her to persecution. Kateri eventually left her village and settled in a Christian village 200 miles away, near Montreal. Having made a vow not to marry, she dedicated her life to prayer and fasting and to teaching others about Christ and serving those in need.

Kateri trusted God to care for all her needs and believed that he would be her source of strength when she faced hardship and suffering. Speaking of the poverty she might face because of the life she had chosen, she said, "I am not my own; I have given myself to Jesus. He must be my only love. The state of helpless poverty that may befall me if I do not marry does not frighten me. . . . If I should become sick and unable to work, then I shall be like the Lord on the cross. He will have mercy on me and help me, I am sure."

Kateri died at age twenty-four. She was the first Native American to be Canonized. We celebrate her feast day on July 14.

Part Review

1. How does God's response to Job help us to understand suffering?

2. What is the deep spiritual truth about suffering and sacrifice that is accepted by disciples of Christ?

3. What are some biblical passages that address the topic of suffering?

4. How does the example of Jesus Christ show us that the willingness to accept sacrifice and suffering is not foolish or a sign of weakness?

5. What are some keys to developing the hope and strength necessary to accept sacrifice and unite our suffering with the Passion of Christ?

6. What is the gift of fortitude?

Prayer and the Paschal Mystery

Part 1

The Fundamentals of Prayer

There is a unity that exists in the Christian faith that shows itself in the natural connections between the truths that have been revealed by God and our practice of the faith. This student book started with an overview of God's great plan of salvation that begins at Creation and leads to the Final Judgment. The heart of this plan is the Passion, death, Resurrection, and Ascension of Jesus Christ, the Paschal Mystery. We then considered how we as disciples of Jesus Christ are called to unite our own lives to his, to participate in his priestly, prophetic, and kingly ministry.

This section takes it one step further. How do we join our efforts to Christ's saving work? How do we move from theory of Christianity to the practice of Christian living? How do we move from knowing about God to knowing God, to developing an intimate relationship with the Father, the Son, and the Holy Spirit? The answers to these questions lie in the unity of faith that connects the Paschal Mystery to prayer. Through prayer God is continuously calling every human being into relationship. Salvation history can be thought of as the unfolding of a relationship of prayer: God calls us into full communion with him and we call out to God in search of his love and truth.

The topics covered in this part are:

41 Why We Pray

Article

If you made a list of ways to develop good friendships, what would it include? Following are some things many people would include on such a list:

- Make time for your friend.
- Talk about things that are important, such as hopes and dreams.
- Do things together, or just hang out.
- Listen to your friend.
- Seek reconciliation and forgiveness when there has been a break in the relationship.

These and other facets of making and keeping strong friendships also apply to another important relationship— the deep, personal relationship we develop with God through prayer.

Prayer Defined

When you were young, you learned to talk by imitating someone else. Sounds and words gradually became yours, and you gained skill at stringing them into phrases and then sentences to express thoughts. This process carries over into prayer. The family should be the first place in which we learn to pray. You probably first learned to talk to God using prayers you were taught. These memorized prayers helped you to express a child's faith. As you grew older, you most likely expanded the ways in which you prayed. You began to

Catholic Wisdom

Being Prayerful Is More Than Saying Prayers

If prayer is simply communication with God, it can go on continually. . . . There is no reason why we should not be able to communicate with God in and through every-thing we do.

(Br. David Steindl-Rast, OSB)

It is possible to offer fervent prayer even while walking in public or strolling alone, or seated in your shop . . . while buying or selling . . . or even while cooking.

(Saint John Chrysostom)

also use your own words in prayer to express who you are, what you think, how you feel, and what you need. But prayer is more than talking to God; we must also spend time in silence to hear God's voice in our lives.

Words are an important part of **prayer,** but just as relationships are more than words, so is prayer more than words. A classic definition of *prayer* is that "prayer is the raising of one's mind and heart to God or the requesting of good things from God" (Saint John Damascene, *De fide orth.* 3, 24: J. P. Migne, ed., Patrologia Graeca [Paris, 1857–1866] 94, 1089C) (*Catechism of the Catholic Church [CCC]*, 2590). Prayer involves your mind and heart. It includes insight and affection, just like a good friendship. Sometimes when you pray, you might experience insight, like a bright lightbulb turning on in your head. More often when you raise your mind to God in prayer, your intellect is shaped so gradually and gently that you notice the change only over time, much like you come to appreciate, years later, the way a good friend or teacher has influenced your thinking. Prayer is also more a matter of the heart. When you allow yourself to open your heart in friendship to God, you will find yourself experiencing God's love in many different ways. When this happens you experience the power of prayer to heal you and to help you to become more loving in all your relationships.

prayer
Lifting up of one's mind and heart to God in praise, petition, thanksgiving, and intercession; communication with God in a relationship of love.

Everyone Is Called to Prayer

When you really want to get to know someone, it is easy to get caught up in worrying about saying the right words and doing the right things. You can probably think of a time when you tried to impress someone else, but you ended up neither getting to know the person nor feeling like yourself. Hopefully you have learned that the best person to be when you are making friends is yourself. The same is true in prayer. Prayer is far less about the right words and techniques and far more about being who God made us to be: people who desire to be in relationship with the One who called us into existence. Everyone is called to prayer. This is because the desire for God is built into us; it is a response to God who first and tirelessly calls us to encounter him through prayer. It's like picking up the phone to call a friend and finding her or him already on the line, having called you first. In prayer God reveals himself to you, and

The Lord's Prayer

The Lord's Prayer has a central place in the prayer life of the Church. This is because it comes to us directly from Jesus and it lays the foundation for all our desires in the Christian life. The Lord's Prayer is the quintessential or perfect example of prayer, which is why we pray it at liturgical celebrations, including every celebration of the Eucharist. When we pray the Lord's Prayer, the Holy Spirit gives life to the words in our hearts and brings us into communion with God—the Father, the Son, and the Holy Spirit. In giving us the Lord's Prayer, Jesus communicated to us the value of prayer for our lives.

you learn about yourself. This reciprocal call between God and humankind has been going on throughout the whole of salvation history. Prayer is a central way God has revealed himself to humankind and shown us who we are.

To assist us in prayer, the Church offers us many opportunities to pray and to learn about prayer. We are invited to pray regularly through daily prayers, the Liturgy of the Hours, Sunday Eucharist, and the feasts of the liturgical year. Many parishes have prayer groups, and prayer is a regular part of parish meetings and activities. Use these opportunities to make prayer a regular part of your life as you seek to grow in holiness and in communion with God. ✞

© Christopher Futcher/istockphoto.com

"I say to you, if two of you agree on earth about anything for which they are to pray, it shall be granted to them by my heavenly Father. For where two or three are gathered together in my name, there am I in the midst of them" (Matthew 18:19-20).

Article 42 The Forms of Prayer

Friendships are based on many things, and you would probably agree that friends bring out different aspects of your personality. Although each friendship brings out a part of you, you probably aren't comfortable sharing everything about yourself with everyone.

The really wonderful thing about prayer is that it is *the* relationship in which you can share all of yourself and know you are loved. No part of you is out of range of the Holy Spirit. God wants to be in relationship with you in every aspect of your life—in all your concerns, gifts, faults, and feelings. The Holy Spirit instructs the Church in the life of prayer, inspiring new expressions of the same basic prayer forms. This gives rise to different forms of prayer—blessing (and adoration), petition, intercession, thanksgiving, and praise—that connect to different times and situations in your life. In this article we learn more about each of these prayer forms.

blessing
A prayer asking God to care for a particular person, place, or activity. A simple blessing is usually made with the Sign of the Cross.

adoration
The prayerful acknowledgment that God is God and Creator of all that is.

Blessing and Adoration

The prayer form **blessing** is a two-step movement. First God gives us a gift, and then we respond with joy and gratitude. If you have ever watched the loving exchange between a parent and an infant, you have glimpsed the basic rhythm of blessing. The parent, who provides for the baby's every need, pours care and devotion over the child. The infant, rejoicing in a love that it can barely fathom, coos and squeals with delight. Like a baby's delight, our prayers of blessing in response to God's many gifts ascend in the Holy Spirit through Christ to the Father.

"Blessed is he who comes in the name of the Lord. Hosanna in the highest" is an example of a blessing we pray at Mass. "I will bless the LORD at all times; / praise shall be always in my mouth" (Psalm 34:1) is a blessing from the Psalms. Just remember that it is because God first blesses us that the human heart can in return bless the One who is the source of every blessing.

Adoration is closely related to blessing. When we adore God, we acknowledge that we are creatures before the One who created us. Adoration, which is reserved for God alone (see Exodus 20:2–7), can take the form of joyful song (see Psalm 95:1) or respectful, humbled silence.

In some blessings you or someone else actually invokes God's power and care on another person, place, thing, or undertaking. The gesture or touch that often accompanies these blessings symbolizes the bestowal of God's grace on the receiver. In Numbers 6:22–27 God instructs Aaron to bless the Israelites. The blessing at the end of the Mass, the familiar Irish blessing, and the blessing of animals on the Feast of Saint Francis are other examples of this kind of blessing.

People have things blessed that are an important part of their lives. We thank God for these things and pray that his power and love will protect them.

© Kiko Huesca/epa/Corbis

Petition

The prayer form **petition** is asking God for something you need. At some level most of us know this, and probably make petitions, the most common form of prayer, dozens of times a day without even realizing it. "Help me pass this test!" "Give me a break, Lord!" "God forgive me!" "Lord, tell me what to say!" Petition is prayer's most usual form because it is the most spontaneous. It arises naturally from the depths of our hearts, where we are aware of our relationship with God, where we know we depend on our Creator. In this prayer form, which is also called supplication, we ask, beseech, plead, invoke, cry out, even struggle in prayer.

It is difficult to have an honest conversation with a friend when we've had an argument. This uneasiness often spills over into other relationships, making them uncomfortable as well. Jesus knew this, and in the Sermon on the Mount, he said to be reconciled with others before prayer (see Matthew 5:22–24). Therefore the first movement of petition is always asking forgiveness: acknowledging our shortcomings and turning back to God. The *Kyrie eleison* ("Lord have mercy, Christ have mercy, Lord have mercy"), said at the Mass, is an example of this call to forgiveness as a prerequisite to prayer.

Even when things are going great with our relationships, it can be awkward to ask for things. Jesus had something to say about that. Right after he taught his disciples the Lord's Prayer, he told two parables about prayer that he summarized by saying, "Ask, and it will be given you; search, and you will find; knock, and the door will be opened to you" (Luke 11:9). Pray with confidence and perseverance, he said, and the Father will give you all you need, above all the Holy Spirit. Novenas, prayers for a particular intention, are an example of perseverance. These devotions span nine consecutive days or nine weeks, and are based on the number of days Mary and the Apostles waited for the coming of the Holy Spirit, from the Ascension to Pentecost.

petition
A prayer form in which one asks God for help and forgiveness.

intercession
A prayer on behalf of another person or group.

Intercession

"Put in a good word for me!" In the ordinary circumstances of life, you might speak a supportive word on behalf of a friend to a possible employer, a secret crush, a teacher, or a coach. **Intercession** is a prayer of petition in which you do something very similar. You ask God's help for another person.

Intercessory prayer has great power. When we offer a prayer of intercession, we join our love for another person with God's love for the person we are praying for. If you have ever played with a magnifying glass on a sunny day, you know you can take a ray of sunlight and intensify it by passing it through the glass. Intercessory prayer works in a similar way. You allow your heart to become like a magnifying glass, channeling God's love in a way that will forever change you and the person you are praying for.

thanksgiving
A prayer of gratitude for the gift of life and the gifts of life. Thanksgiving characterizes the prayer of the Church which, in celebrating the Eucharist, offers perfect thanks to the Father through, with, and in Christ, in the unity of the Holy Spirit.

praise
A prayer of acknowledgment that God is God, giving God glory not for what he does, but simply because he is.

Just as putting in a good word for a friend comes quite naturally, it is easy to pray for those who are closest to you. Intercession invites you to broaden your circle of concern, to see yourself as part of something much greater. In prayers that reach out to Church and world leaders, and to the lonely, sick, and forgotten people throughout the world, every baptized person can work for the coming of the Kingdom. These more expansive prayers are also the basis for the prayers of intercession during Mass.

You might ask, "But what about Jesus' command to pray for our enemies and those who persecute us?" (see Matthew 5:43–44). These can be the hardest prayers to offer with a sincere heart. When we stretch ourselves to pray for someone we are in conflict with or for someone who has hurt us, we are affirming our belief that no person or concern is outside the love and care of God.

Thanksgiving

In **thanksgiving** we remember that we are creatures and God is our Creator. The more we pray in thanksgiving, the more we grow in awareness that all we have comes to us as a gift from God's abundant love. The Greek word *eucharist* means "thanksgiving." Early Christians prayed with a grateful spirit in the "breaking of bread" (see Acts of the Apostles 2:42–47). At the Mass, Catholics join in this prayer of thanksgiving with Christ and offer back to the Father all he has accomplished in Christ. Many people offer their personal prayers with the prayer of the Church by spending the quiet moments after the Communion Rite in thanksgiving.

Saint Paul tells us the real test of a grateful heart is this: "In all circumstances give thanks" (1 Thessalonians 5:18). This may sound a little phony to you, but Paul isn't telling you to put on a false front. What he means is that you can have confidence that God is loving you, even in the middle of difficulties, even when you can't see the purpose for your suffering, even when no end is in sight. Such gratitude involves deep faith in the Paschal Mystery—the mystery that life and growth come through death and suffering. Through the lens of the Paschal Mystery, broken friendships, addictions, illness, and death become windows into the vastness of God's abiding love, and the Christian heart wells up in gratitude.

The Divine Praises

The divine praises are a form of adoration. These praises name some of the wonderful blessings of our faith. Pray them from time to time as part of your adoration of God.

Blessed be God.

Blessed be his holy name.

Blessed be Jesus Christ, true God and true man.

Blessed be the name of Jesus.

Blessed be his most sacred heart.

Blessed be his Most Precious Blood.

Blessed be Jesus in the most holy sacrament of the altar.

Blessed be the Holy Spirit, the Paraclete.

Blessed be the great mother of God, Mary most holy.

Blessed be her holy and immaculate conception.

Blessed be her glorious assumption.

Blessed be the name of Mary, virgin and mother.

Blessed be Saint Joseph, her most chaste spouse.

Blessed be God in his angels and in his saints.

Praise

Praise embraces all other forms of prayer and carries them to God, who is our source and goal. Praise is the form of prayer that expresses our love for God simply because God *is*. You know if you have felt this natural, self-forgetful kind of love for God welling up in you for no particular reason. When this happens the Holy Spirit is working in you to inspire you to glorify God. Saint Paul told the Ephesians to "be filled with the Spirit, addressing one another [in] psalms and hymns and spiritual songs, singing and playing to the Lord in your hearts" (Ephesians 5:19).

Praise often finds its expression in music. The *Gloria* we sing at the Mass echoes the angels' song of praise that beckoned the shepherds to worship the newborn Jesus. In this hymn we sing, "We praise you, we bless you, . . . we give you thanks for your great glory." The thanks we offer in the *Gloria* is not for what God has done but simply because he exists and is so glorious. Many other traditional prayers express praise. *Alleluia* literally means "praise the Lord." It comes to

doxology
The Christian prayers of praise that are usually directed to the Trinity.

us from our Jewish roots and has been the Easter cry of the Church from the time the first Christians celebrated Christ's victory over death. Many of the Psalms are prayers of praise. *Doxology* is a word for the Christian prayers of praise that are usually directed to the Trinity. ✝

How is praise a part of your prayer life? When and where do you offer your praise and thanksgiving to God?

Article 43 The Expressions of Prayer

An earlier article reflected on Jesus' prayer life and what he had to teach us about prayer. Our prayer is primarily addressed to the Father. We pray in the name of Jesus, the Divine Son, to our Father, guided by and empowered by the Holy Spirit. Through Sacred Tradition, the living transmission of our faith, the Holy Spirit teaches us how to pray. Tradition guides us to the many sources available for prayer: the Sacred Scriptures, the liturgy of the Church, and the theological virtues of faith, hope, and charity. Many of our prayers come out of the Bible or are based on biblical passages or events, including Mass prayers, the Lord's Prayer, the Hail Mary, and the *Angelus*.

Tradition also teaches us about the three major expressions in a life of prayer: vocal prayer, meditation, and contemplation. These three expressions in some ways can be likened to the way communication develops in courtship and Marriage. At first the man and woman share about all the things that are happening in their lives; they talk about their values, their goals, their day-to-day thoughts. As the friendship deepens, they also begin to reflect on their relationship; they have greater awareness of each other and their love for each other. At some point in their life together, they simply enjoy each other's presence, their love connecting them without the need for words. The expressions of prayer are built upon an open and sincere heart as we deepen our relationship with God.

The Light of the Spirit

Saint John Chrysostom (AD 347–407) is a Doctor of the Church who was famous for his preaching. *Chrysostom* literally means "golden-mouthed." Here is a portion of a homily he gave on prayer:

> As the eyes of the body are enlightened when they see light, so our spirit, when it is intent on God, is illumined by his infinite light. I do not mean the prayer of outward observance but prayer from the heart, not confined to fixed times or periods but continuous throughout the day and night. . . . Prayer is the light of the spirit, true knowledge of God, mediating between God and man. The spirit, raised up to heaven by prayer, clings to God with the utmost tenderness; like a child crying tearfully for its mother, it craves the milk that God provides. . . . One who tastes this food is set on fire with an eternal longing for the Lord: his spirit burns as in a fire of the utmost intensity.

© Araldo de Luca/CORBIS

Expressions of Prayer

Vocal Prayer

vocal prayer
A prayer that is spoken aloud or silently, such as the Lord's Prayer.

meditation
A form of prayer involving a variety of methods and techniques, in which one engages the mind, imagination, and emotions to focus on a particular truth, biblical theme, or other spiritual matter.

When you want to get to know someone, you might strike up a conversation. At first you usually focus on simple things: school, music, sports. As you get to know each other better, you begin to share about topics of greater importance: your beliefs, your worries, your dreams for the future. **Vocal prayer,** which uses words either spoken aloud or recited silently, is similar to this kind of sharing because it focuses on your conversation with God, which grows over time. Memorized prayer is the first way most people learn to pray vocally. Children usually learn these prayers in their families and in religious education classes. These classic prayers serve us throughout our lifetime and are important and appropriate at every stage of spiritual development.

You will probably also find it helpful to pray to God in your own words. God wants us to share our joys and trials, hopes and frustrations. We can be angry with God, confused, or just plain goofy. The Gospels show that Jesus shouted at God both in joy (see Matthew 11:25–26) and in agony on the cross (see Mark 15:37). Praying memorized prayers and praying in our own words are both important forms of vocal prayer.

Creating a space to pray in your home is a reminder to make prayer a regular part of your life.

© Macduff Everton/CORBIS

Meditation

Meditation is a term used broadly and somewhat loosely. The word goes back to a Greek root meaning "care, study, and exercise." You can tell by these meanings that in its truest sense, meditation involves real activity. The *Catechism of the Catholic Church* uses the active word *mobilize* to describe the use of thoughts, imagination, emotions, and desires in meditation. When you meditate you use these faculties to ponder God's presence and activity in your life and in the world, to discover the movements that stir your heart, and to say, "Lord, I want you to be the focus of my life."

There are many and varied methods of meditation. Catholics and other Christians often use the Scriptures as a springboard to meditation, as in ***lectio divina,*** which was introduced in the previous student book in this series, *The Bible: The Living Word of God.* Liturgical texts of the day or season, holy writings, the Rosary, icons, and all creation are other doors through which you can enter into meditation. Regardless of how you enter, Christian meditation is not Zen or Eastern meditation or relaxation or mere psychological activity, but a path to the knowledge of the love of Christ and union with him.

Contemplative Prayer

Like *meditation,* the word ***contemplation*** has held different meanings throughout the history of spirituality. This kind

lectino divina

A Latin term meaning "divine reading." *Lectio divina* is a form of meditative prayer focused on a Scripture passage. It involves repetitive readings and periods of reflection and can serve as either private or communal prayer.

contemplation

A form of wordless prayer in which one is fully focused on the presence of God; sometimes defined as "resting in God."

Pray It!

Lord, What Do You Want Me To Do?

Through meditation we can discover the stirrings of our hearts and gain insight about what God wants us to do. There are many ways to meditate, but here are some simple steps for getting started:

1. Select a focus for your meditation, such as a Scripture passage, a spiritual writing, or an event from the life of Christ.
2. Choose a quiet place that is as free from distraction as possible.
3. Begin by assuming a posture conducive to prayer, such as kneeling or sitting.
4. Recall that you are in the holy presence of God and ask for his help in understanding his will for your life.
5. Turn your attention to the selected focus of your meditation, allowing it to engage your thoughts, imagination, and emotions. For example, if you are meditating on an event in the life of Christ, try to imagine yourself in the event.
6. Conclude with a prayer of thanksgiving.

Keep in mind that meditation is most fruitful when practiced on a regular basis. Practiced over time, meditation can deepen your faith and strengthen your relationship with Christ.

of union, or awareness of oneness, is the central element of *mysticism*, another term used to describe experiences of profound union with God. What is consistent in descriptions of contemplation is that it always has to do with deep awareness of the presence of God; this awareness is arrived at not by rational thought but by love. It is the experience of oneness with God that Jesus speaks about in the Gospel of John, with words like "Remain in me" (15:4) and "I in them" (17:26). Contemplation is union with the indwelling Christ that takes place in the heart at prayer.

You might be thinking, "Okay, really holy people can do this, not me!" Remember, we are all called to holiness in the ordinary events of our everyday lives. It doesn't take holiness to pray, but prayer will make you holier. Try not to think of contemplation as something to "do." It is God who loves you and draws near to you. Contemplation is God's gift to you, and you can accept it only in humility. The Psalms offer an image that conveys the truly simple nature of contemplative prayer. Think of it as climbing into God's lap, like a child rests in his mother's arms (see Psalm 131). It is simply dwelling in God's love. ✝

Article 44 Overcoming Obstacles to Prayer

You would think that if prayer were so essential, it would also be easy. Prayer can seem easy, but developing a consistent and regular prayer life is often challenging. Like any good habit, it can be difficult to get going, but once you develop the habit, it is easy to maintain. Prayer brings God's peace and joy into our lives, and once we have had a taste, we will want to keep coming back for more.

But as you may have already discovered in life, even good habits can die out over time. Those who do attempt prayer will sooner or later face other difficulties, particularly the challenges of distraction and periods of dryness. When this happens take heart. Those great saints who said that prayer is a battle learned to fight the battle well and left advice for how to handle these difficulties. We consider some of that advice in this article. Always remember that you are not alone. The Holy Spirit prays with you and will see you through.

Misconceptions about Prayer

A lot of misconceptions exist about prayer. Just as having the wrong idea about a person hinders us in getting to know him or her, having the wrong idea about prayer works against us. Common misconceptions are that prayer is merely a psychological activity or the rattling off of memorized words. This is not part of healthy human relationships and is also not true prayer. Another misconception is that prayer is something that requires expertise. There are no black belts, no *summa cum laude* honors, no five-stars in prayer. Anyone can pray, and you probably already do.

For example, do you ever sit in your room listening to music, caught up in the rhythm and how the verses express your own thoughts and feelings about your relationship with God? Do you ever look at a tiny infant or a beautiful sunset and think, "Way to go, God!" When you are caught in a difficult situation, do you turn to God and ask for help? If you do any of these things, you are already praying. Most people pray at some level, even if it is only occasional and unplanned. What God wants us to do is to be more disciplined and consistent in our prayer—to make him a regular part of our life.

Live It!

Prayer and Holiness

For the Israelites being "holy" was more than just being good. It also means to be different or set apart for service to God. When things are important to us, we set aside a special place or time for them. Activities such as tutoring, music lessons, or sports usually get a specific time in the day or week so that we are sure to attend them regularly. So if holiness is important to us, wouldn't it make sense that we would also set aside regular times to spend in prayer?

Though we can pray anywhere at any time, most saints have found that their growth in holiness is strongly tied to setting aside regular times for prayer. Sunday is a holy day for Christians. We set this day apart from the others so that we can gather to pray as a community. In our personal lives, it is just as important to set aside times in the day for prayer. The morning, before starting the day's activities, is a good time, as well as evening, before closing the day out. We can begin our meals by offering our gratitude for God's gifts. Make yourself more open to the work of God's grace by setting aside time for prayer every day.

Another misconception is over Paul's command to the Thessalonians to "Pray without ceasing" (1 Thessalonians 5:17). This does not mean that every Christian should join a monastery and spend every waking moment in prayer; rather, it means that our whole life should be a prayer, a sign of our communion with God. We do this by remembering that it is always possible to pray, no matter what life may throw at us. We do it by remembering that prayer is a necessity. Without prayer we lose our connection to God and we fall back into a life of sin and unhappiness. And we do it by remembering that prayer and Christian action are two sides of the same coin. Origen, an early Christian thinker, said it like this: "He 'prays without ceasing' who unites his prayer to works and good works to prayer. Only in this way can we consider as realizable the principle of praying without ceasing."

People in monastic life pray the Liturgy of the Hours together several times a day as one way of "praying without ceasing." How is your life a living prayer to God?

© Danny Lehman/CORBIS

Difficulties in Prayer: Distractions and Dryness

Distractions in prayer are similar to what happens when you try to carry on a conversation and keep getting interrupted. Some days it seems the moment you bow in prayer, a dozen alarms go off in your head at once, all calling you away from the relationship of prayer: "Oh, no! I forgot to call Sue!" "I wonder what I should wear to the dance." "I've got to get that job application in by tomorrow." The moment you quiet one distraction, another one pops up, like a game of mental jack-in-the-box.

Spiritual guides tell us that these distractions reveal our preferences and attachments and therefore which master we serve (see Matthew 6:21,24). They advise against hunting down distractions because that is precisely the trap—to get us chasing around instead of praying. Respond just as you would to interruptions in conversation. Turn your focus back to the Lord, with whom you want to be. In doing so

Saint John of the Cross

Saint John of the Cross is a famous Spanish mystic born in 1542. He learned firsthand the meaning of sacrifice; his father was disowned from his wealthy family for marrying a common woman. As a young adult, John joined the Carmelite order, and Saint Teresa of Ávila asked him to help her reform the order through a stricter emphasis on personal prayer and spirituality. Some Carmelites were so threatened by this that they kidnapped John and kept him prisoner. Instead of turning bitter about this, he devoted his life to teaching others to find God through love and prayer.

John was a great spiritual poet. His two most famous works are *Ascent of Mount Carmel* and *Dark Night of the Soul*. In *Dark Night of the Soul*, he encourages Christians who are struggling with spiritual darkness. These are times of difficulty in prayer and even the feeling that you have been abandoned by God. John encourages us to see these as times when our love for God is being purified. Rather than being a negative, the "dark night" is a blessing in disguise, drawing us into closer communion with God.

you demonstrate which master you choose to serve. This is vigilance: constantly seeking God instead of allowing other things to draw you away.

The next difficulty, dryness, is akin to those times in even the best friendship when the spark seems to have faded. You seem to be growing apart; you no longer have as much fun when you are together. Remaining faithful to your friend and exploring new activities together are important if you do not want the friendship to die. In prayer, dryness is experienced as feeling separated from God. When this happens the strength, joy, and peace of prayer run dry, and nothing seems to change the situation. Sometimes these periods of dryness, or darkness, are the gift and work of God, liberating you from imperfections and attachments. If this is the case, keeping faith will see you through.

At other times dryness is the result of a lack of devotion to the relationship. In Marriage couples can focus too much on other things—raising children, earning money, other friends—and grow lax in devotion to each other. The couple has to radically reorient their priorities to mend their Marriage. If our prayer is dry because of lax practice or carelessness of heart, the remedy is conversion. Conversion involves a radical change of heart, turning away from the things that draw us away from God, and returning to God.

All this talk of difficulties may have you feeling discouraged. Listen to this modern-day parable: The Devil takes a man on a tour of Hell and proudly shows off all his storehouses brimming with the seeds of sin. There is lust and jealousy, anger and envy, and so on—a large storehouse for each big sin. But the man points out another storehouse larger by far than all the rest. "What do you keep in there?" he asks. "Oh, that," responds the Devil, "that holds the smallest but most effective seed of all. That is overflowing with seeds of discouragement." Prayer can be such a wonderful and life-giving relationship that you want to take great care not to allow the seeds of discouragement to grow there. Remember, even an infinitesimal seed of faith grows to the size of a mustard tree, whose roots and shade hold back despair, hopelessness, and fear (see Luke 17:5–6). ✞

45 Ignatian Gospel Meditation

Article

Many different schools of Christian **spirituality** offer us valuable guidance in developing our prayer life. These different schools have developed out of the living tradition of prayer in the life of the Church. Guided by the Holy Spirit, many of these schools come from the spiritual insights of particular saints. In this article we look to one of these schools of spirituality, Ignatian spirituality.

One of God's greatest gifts to us is our imagination. Through it we can discover possibilities, break down barriers, and solve problems. People have accomplished amazing things because they dared to imagine the world in new and different ways. Christians are able to endure the sacrifices needed to give witness to the Gospel because we can imagine the complete fulfillment of the Kingdom of God. But have you ever considered using your imagination for prayer?

The power and beauty of the human imagination were not lost on Saint Ignatius of Loyola. While recovering from a war injury, he spent months in spiritual reading. Some of the books he read encouraged him to imagine himself being part of the scenes in the Gospel story. This use of the imagination for prayer and discernment deeply affected Ignatius, and he took this idea and developed a whole series of spiritual exercises based on it. Imagining yourself as part of a Gospel story can be a very powerful way of hearing the voice of God.

spirituality

In general, the values, actions, attitudes, and behaviors that characterize a person's relationship with God and others. In particular, it refers to different schools of Christian prayer and action.

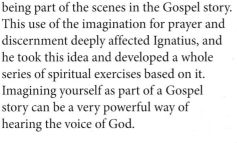

Saint Ignatius gave up the vanity of courtly life after discovering the power of the Gospel and the peace it brought him. His methods for prayer became one of the Church's most well known schools of Christian spirituality.

© Leonard de Selva/CORBIS

The Method

Saint Ignatius developed a method of prayer that uses the imagination to immerse the person praying into a story from the Bible. With this method you visualize in your mind the details of the Gospel story. It can be thought of as a meditation that may even draw you into contemplation. As the story comes to life in your imagination, you are brought to a personal and real encounter with Jesus in the present moment. Here is a suggested format to follow for Ignatian Gospel meditation:

1. Prepare yourself for prayer by assuming a comfortable position and allowing yourself to become silent. Select a passage from the Scriptures with which to pray. It is usually best to begin with the Gospels, because the details and storyline are especially suited to this method. With some experience you will be able to spot other passages in the Scriptures that also work well.

2. Read the passage through once, paying special attention to the characters and the concrete details: What does this place look, feel, smell, and sound like? Who is there? What action unfolds? What words are spoken? You may wish to reread the passage several times to absorb all the details.

3. Next, enter into the story in your imagination, just as if you were there. Employ your senses to allow the details of the story to come alive. Listen, taste, feel, smell, and see all you can. Either be yourself or imagine yourself as one of the people in the story. Converse and interact with the people in the story. Allow the story to unfold in your imagination without changing any of the essential details from the Bible passage.

4. As you experience the story, pay careful attention to all your reactions, all that you are feeling and thinking.

5. Respond to this experience in prayerful conversation with Jesus.

Try It

As an example, let's pray with the passage in John 21:1–14, where the resurrected Jesus appears to his disciples while they are fishing on the Sea of Tiberius (Sea of Galilee). You imagine the rocking of the boat as the nets are thrown out, the warmth of the sun, each person in the boat with you, and the quiet conversation as you ponder the meaning of Jesus' death, the empty tomb, and the appearances of your Risen Lord. You work the nets without any success. What are you talking about as you do this? Then a stranger appears on shore at dawn and tells you to cast your net again. You do so and the net is so full that you cannot even pull it into the boat. What feelings are you experiencing as this happens? Then John and Peter recognize the figure as Jesus, and Peter enthusiastically jumps into the water so he can be the first to shore. You all come in dragging the full net behind the boat. Jesus himself cooks some fish and feeds you fish and bread for breakfast. What feelings are deep in your heart? What kind of conversation do you have with Jesus? How will this experience affect your life?

You might be thinking: "This is all just imagination. It isn't real!" Recall that the Scriptures are the "living Word." Those who pray with this method have very real encounters with Jesus and find that in the experience, God touches them. They are comforted, healed, and challenged by the living Christ as they meet him through the doorway of the imagination. They find meaning in the story that they might have overlooked before.

Passages for Ignatian Gospel Meditation

Though any Gospel passage can be used for Ignatian Gospel meditation, there are particular passages that Christians have found speak to them very powerfully using this type of prayer. Here are some of them:

- Luke 2:1–20 (the birth of Jesus)
- Matthew 4:18–22 (the call of the first disciples)
- Mark 8:27–38 (Peter recognizes that Jesus is the Messiah)
- John 13:1–17 (Jesus washes the disciples' feet)
- Matthew 26:57–75 (Jesus before the Sanhedrin, Peter's denial of Jesus)
- Mark 15:15–41 (the death of Jesus)
- Luke 24:13–32 (the Risen Jesus appears to two disciples)
- John 20:24–31 (Jesus appears to Thomas)

As the living Word of God, the Scriptures have a unique contribution to make in the practice of prayer. *Lectio divina* and Ignatian Gospel meditation are simple ways to start a conversation with God's Word and keep it going. If you aren't in dialogue with God's Word, try these methods when you pray today. ✝

You can use images as an aid to Ignatian meditation. Use this image of the story in John 21:1–14 to help you imagine being in the story.

Part Review

1. What is prayer? Why must we pray?

2. How is the prayer form petition different from the prayer form intercession?

3. Describe some different types of vocal prayer.

4. What is consistent in descriptions of contemplative prayer?

5. Describe some of the misconceptions people have about prayer.

6. How can you overcome being distracted while praying?

7. How can our imagination be helpful in prayer? How did Saint Ignatius of Loyola use imagination when praying with the Scriptures?

Part 2

Praying the Triduum

In the previous part, we looked primarily at the connection between the Paschal Mystery and personal prayer. Now we turn our attention to the connection between the Paschal Mystery and the liturgy, which is the Church's official, public, communal prayer. In particular, we look at the Easter Triduum, the three-day celebration that is the heart of the liturgical year.

Every Eucharist makes the saving sacrifice of Jesus present to us. And the liturgical year commemorates the various aspects of the Paschal Mystery in an annual cycle. But the liturgies of Holy Thursday, Good Friday, and Easter commemorate in a unique way the Passion and Resurrection of Jesus Christ. In our journey to holiness, the Easter Triduum offers us a kind of annual Paschal Mystery retreat. These liturgies are a special gift to be treasured and celebrated with the Church, the Body of Christ.

The topics covered in this part are:

46 Introduction to the Triduum

Article

Most people make an effort to celebrate the Fourth of July, Thanksgiving, New Year's Eve, or whatever national holidays are important in their country. God created us to be in relationship, and holidays unite us as citizens with a common heritage. Christians, who are first and foremost citizens of the Kingdom of God, have "holidays" too (only we call them holy days). Our celebration of the holy day liturgies binds us together and strengthens us as the Body of Christ.

The Lord's Day and the Liturgical Year

The most fundamental and foundational holy day is the Lord's Day. We celebrate this day on Sunday, in honor of Christ's Resurrection, which occurred on Sunday morning. We keep the Lord's Day holy by participating in the Eucharist (the Mass) and taking time for rest, prayer, and family.

Sunday is the foundation of the **liturgical year,** which begins with the First Sunday of Advent. During the liturgical year, we remember and celebrate God the Father's saving plan as it is revealed through the life of his Son, Jesus Christ. In Advent we patiently wait for Jesus' birth, during the Christmas season we celebrate his Incarnation, in Lent we remember his call to a life of holiness and sacrifice, and during the Easter Triduum and Easter season we celebrate his suffering, death, and Resurrection. Forty days after Easter, we recall Christ's Ascension into Heaven. Ten days after that, we rejoice in the gift of the Holy Spirit at Pentecost. During Ordinary Time we ponder our call to live as disciples while waiting for Christ's final return as Lord of Lords and King of Kings.

The Liturgy and the Paschal Mystery

Liturgy is the Church's public, communal, and official worship. The Eucharist is the central liturgy of the Church and the basis for most other liturgical celebrations. The other six Sacraments are also liturgies, and so are the **Liturgy of the Hours** and Catholic funerals. But a group prayer service is not a liturgy, because it is not an official worship service of the Church.

liturgical year
The annual cycle of religious feasts and seasons that forms the context for the Church's worship. During the liturgical year, we remember and celebrate God the Father's saving plan as it is revealed through the life of his Son, Jesus Christ.

liturgy
The Church's official, public, communal prayer. It is God's work, in which the People of God participate. The Church's most important liturgy is the Eucharist, or the Mass.

Liturgy of the Hours
Also known as the Divine Office, the official public, daily prayer of the Catholic Church. The Divine Office provides standard prayers, Scripture readings, and reflections at regular hours throughout the day.

Sacrament

An efficacious and visible sign of God's invisible grace, instituted by Christ. The Seven Sacraments are Baptism, the Eucharist, Confirmation, Penance and Reconciliation, Anointing of the Sick, Matrimony, and Holy Orders.

Triduum

The three-day period of the liturgical year that begins with the Mass of the Lord's Supper on Holy Thursday and ends with evening prayer on Easter Sunday.

It is helpful to define some terms. The word *liturgy* is taken from the Greek word *liturgia*, which means "a public work" or "service on behalf of the people." *The liturgy or the sacred liturgy* refers to the overall idea of Catholic official worship, but *a liturgy* usually refers to a specific Mass or sacramental celebration. *Liturgical* describes anything related to the liturgy. A *liturgical celebration or ritual* is another name for a Mass or a Baptism or any other specific liturgy. A *liturgist* is a person who studies, researches, and teaches in the field of liturgy and who may also plan and coordinate liturgical celebrations.

The sacred liturgy is Trinitarian. In the liturgy we bless and worship God the Father as the source of the blessings of creation and salvation. The greatest blessing the Father has bestowed on us is the gift of his Son, Jesus Christ, through whom we have become the adopted children of God.

Jesus Christ plays a central role, because he not only gave us the sacred liturgy but also makes himself present through the liturgy, which is another way of saying that the liturgy is sacramental—that is, like a Sacrament. A **Sacrament,** such as the Seven Sacraments of the Church, makes Christ's presence real. The Church herself is like a sacrament because it makes Christ's saving presence available to all people through the proclamation of the Word and the celebration of the Sacraments. Through the sacred liturgy, the Church is already participating in the divine liturgy, as a foretaste of Heaven. Thus the liturgy is the work

© Wojtek Kryczka/istockphoto.com

of both Christ—the head—and the Church—the Body—of
Christ.

The Holy Spirit prepares us to receive Christ in the
liturgy and reveals Christ's presence in the community, the
Scriptures, and the physical signs of liturgical celebrations.
Through his transforming power, the Paschal Mystery is real
and active in the liturgy, bringing us into deeper communion with Christ and with one another. The Holy Spirit gives
us the grace to live as disciples of Christ, participating in his
saving work.

It is important that you understand these last points.
The liturgy is not just a celebration of past events. It makes
the Paschal Mystery available to us right now, just as it was
available to the original disciples and Apostles. Of course
Christ is close to us all the time, but he is available to us in
a unique way through the liturgy and the Sacraments of the
Church, especially the Eucharist.

The Significance of the Triduum

Triduum (pronounced TRI-doo-um) literally means "three
days." It can refer to any three days set apart for prayer or
some other special service. But it usually describes the Easter
Triduum, the three holy days that are at the center of the
Church's liturgical year. The **Triduum** begins with the Mass
of the Lord's Supper on Holy Thursday night, continues
with the Celebration of the Lord's Passion on Good Friday

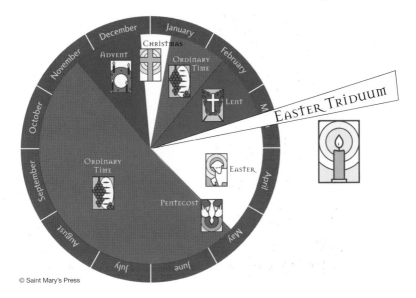

© Saint Mary's Press

The Triduum and Jesus' Final Days

The Gospel readings of the liturgies of the Triduum roughly parallel the final events in Jesus' mission. The Triduum liturgies are not meant to reenact these events but to help us to remember them and sacramentally celebrate them.

Liturgy	Corresponding Events in Jesus' Life
Holy Thursday	Jesus washes the Apostles' feet, institutes the Eucharist at the Last Supper
Good Friday	the Passion (suffering and death) of Jesus
Easter Vigil and Easter Day	discovery of the empty tomb, Resurrection of Christ

afternoon, reaches its climax with the Easter Vigil on Holy Saturday night, and ends with evening prayer on Easter Sunday (so it actually encompasses three twenty-four-hour periods over four days). The liturgies of the Triduum form one continuous celebration, each liturgy picking up where the previous one leaves off; we follow Jesus' Paschal journey from the Last Supper, through his arrest, torture, and Crucifixion, to the joy of the empty tomb and his Resurrection.

The liturgies of the Triduum are unique in their celebration. They are filled with special signs and symbolic actions that help us to meditate on the wonder and glory of God's saving plan, culminating in the Paschal Mystery. The worshipping community has many opportunities to actively participate and to be drawn in to the mystery and drama of the final days of Christ's earthly ministry. It is a shame that many Catholics miss these wonderful liturgies—a gift of the Holy Spirit to renew and strengthen our faith. Even though you are obligated to attend the Mass only on Easter, make whatever sacrifices necessary to attend all these liturgies. ✝

Article 47 Holy Thursday

All through Lent we have been seeking to deepen our participation with Christ's ministry through prayer, fasting, and acts of charity (almsgiving). On Passion (Palm) Sunday we enter into Holy Week by recalling Christ's suffering and death, his sacrifice to save us from sin and death. Think of this time as a personal retreat, a time when you can meditate on Christ's suffering, death, and Resurrection and enter more deeply into these great mysteries. It will require you to move out of your ordinary schedule and obligations as much as possible and enter into sacred time and space for these three holy days. This article and the next two will help you to make the most of this opportunity.

The Church Prays

O God, who have called us to participate
in this most sacred Supper,
in which your Only Begotten Son,
when about to hand himself over to death,
entrusted to the Church a sacrifice new for all eternity,
the banquet of his love, grant, we pray,
that we may draw from so great a mystery,
the fullness of charity and of life.
Through our Lord Jesus Christ, your Son,
who lives and reigns with you in the unity of the Holy Spirit,
one God, for ever and ever.

(Opening prayer from the Mass of the Lord's Supper)

Holy Thursday, the first day of the Triduum, is filled with anticipation at the start of the Triduum. The Triduum begins in the evening, when we celebrate the Mass of the Lord's Supper. We keep watch with Jesus as the Church remembers the glory and heartbreak of the final night of his earthly ministry. Holy Thursday is often the day when all the clergy of your diocese, along with representatives from every parish, gather at the Cathedral with your bishop for the **Chrism Mass,** although this Mass may also be celebrated at an earlier time, such as the Thursday before Holy Thursday. At this liturgy, diocesan priests renew their promises to their bishop, and the bishop blesses the **Oil of the Catechumens** and the **Oil of the Sick** and consecrates the **Sacred Chrism** that will be used in every parish throughout the next year.

Liturgical Highlights

The Mass of the Lord's Supper is a Mass, but there are some special rituals that make it quite different from Sunday Mass. Knowing their meaning will help you to celebrate them more fully.

The Presentation of the Oils

At the beginning of the liturgy, the Oil of the Catechumens, the Oil of the Sick, and the Sacred Chrism are brought up in procession by three members of the parish community. This represents your local parish's connection with the diocese and the universal Church. These oils will be used in the Sacraments of Baptism, Confirmation, and Anointing of the Sick. As the oils are brought up, remember your bishop in prayer; he is entrusted with the challenging task of serving all the people of the diocese. Also pray for the people who will be anointed with these sacred oils throughout the year; pray that they will know Christ's saving, healing, and loving presence through these Sacraments.

At the Holy Thursday liturgy, imagine Christ washing your feet. Let his example inspire you to a life of humble service.

© Arte & Immagini srl/CORBIS

The Washing of Feet

Following the homily the priest or priests of the parish washes the feet of some parish members. This is done in memory of Jesus' act of washing the disciples' feet and his command, "I have given you a model to follow, so that as I have done for you, you should also do" (John 13:15). During this ritual, reflect on who has been a servant in your life and on whom God has called you to serve. Pray for those people.

The Dismissal of the Elect

If your parish has adults who are going to be received into the Church at the Easter Vigil, they are dismissed before the intercessions. The Triduum is especially meaningful for them, for it is the last stage in their process of becoming full members of the Body of Christ. Let their faith and commitment to Christ and the Church inspire you to deeper commitment to our faith.

The Collection for the Poor

The collection taken on Holy Thursday is different from typical Sunday collections. It is solely for the needs of the poor; the food and money collected does not go toward parish expenses. Some parishes participate in Operation Rice Bowl, which is organized by Catholic Charities. Some parishes encourage people to bring bags of food for the hungry in their community. Encourage your family to participate, and help out with your family's donation. Remembering that Christ calls us to sacrifice for the needs of others, make your donation more than just pocket change. If possible, help to increase the collection total as a sign of your commitment to sacrificial service of those most in need.

The Transfer of the Eucharist

Because there is no Liturgy of the Eucharist on Good Friday, enough bread is consecrated on Holy Thursday for both the Holy Thursday and Good Friday liturgies. At the end of the Mass of the Lord's Supper, the Body of Christ that will be used on Good Friday is transferred to a separate location, called the reservation chapel, where it remains until the Good Friday liturgy. In some parishes the congregation joins in the procession, following the priest, who is carrying the Body of Christ. Recall that after the Last Supper, Jesus

Holy Thursday

The beginning of the Easter Triduum, starting with the evening celebration of the Mass of the Lord's Supper.

Chrism Mass

A special Mass usually celebrated during Holy Week in each diocese. During the Mass the bishop blesses the sacred oils and consecrates the Sacred Chrism used throughout the year, and diocesan priests renew their promises to their bishop.

Oil of the Catechumens

Blessed olive oil used to anoint those preparing for Baptism.

Oil of the Sick

Blessed olive oil used in the Sacrament of Anointing of the Sick to anoint the forehead and hands of people who are seriously ill or near death.

Sacred Chrism

Perfumed olive oil that has been consecrated. It is used for anointing in the Sacraments of Baptism, Confirmation, and Holy Orders.

and his disciples walked to the garden at Gethsemane, where he asked the disciples to stay awake and pray with him. In memory of this, many people stay in the reservation chapel to pray with Jesus, or they come back later that night to do so. This is a wonderful and special time to meditate and pray in the presence of Jesus.

The Paschal Fast

Following the Mass of the Lord's Supper, we begin the Paschal Fast. The Church calls for us to abstain from meat and to eat only one full meal on Good Friday, and if we eat other meals that day, they should be less than another full meal. But this is a minimal requirement. Some choose to fast all the way to the Easter Vigil on Saturday night, eating very little until that time.

Fasting, along with prayer and almsgiving, is a penitential practice that expresses our conversion—the turning of our lives away from sin and toward God. Fasting prepares us for participation in liturgical feasts, but it also helps us to control our instincts and act virtuously. Fasting during the Triduum builds our anticipation for the joyous celebration of the Easter Vigil, when we will feast on the Word of God and the Body and Blood of Christ.

Live It!

Remembering the Triduum at Home

M any families have a home altar as a center for family prayer. This can be a simple table displaying a crucifix, Bible, or other religious symbols. If your family does not have one, suggest it to your parents or keep one in your own room. A bedside stand could work perfectly.

At the time of the Triduum, pictures, colors, and symbols can act as reminders of each liturgical celebration. For example, on Holy Thursday you could put out some bread, oil, water, and a collection bowl for the poor on a simple white cloth. On Good Friday a crucifix and perhaps some thorns from a bush laid on a red cloth would set the appropriate mood. For Saturday evening and Sunday, on a gold or white cloth you could display a picture or statue of the Risen Jesus along with a large rock that symbolizes the stone rolled away from the empty tomb. You can visually bring a prayerful mood for the Triduum into your home in many creative ways.

Entering into Sacred Time

Following are suggestions for ways you can more fully enter into the celebration of the Paschal Mystery, beginning with Holy Thursday:

- If you do nothing else, be sure to attend the Mass of the Lord's Supper. Find out the time it begins and mark it on your calendar. Encourage your family and friends to go too.

- Decide what you are going to contribute in the collection for the poor. You may wish to save up for this during the Lenten season by saving money you would have spent on food, soft drinks, clothes, music, or games. Talk with your family to make this a family effort.

- Before or after the Mass of the Lord's Supper, take time to read and reflect on the readings for the Mass: Exodus 12:1–14, Psalm 116, 1 Corinthians 11:23–26, John 13:1–15. The Gospel reading is an excellent reading to use for Ignatian Gospel meditation.

- Make a commitment to fast, and free yourself of distractions for the next three days. Decide what you will allow yourself to eat, and then stick to your commitment. Make a decision not to watch television or use the computer or your phone for anything that is not absolutely necessary.

- Spend an hour with the Blessed Sacrament in the reservation chapel on Thursday night. Jesus' presence in the Eucharistic species is real and substantial. You can talk with him in prayer, read the Scriptures (the Church recommends Psalm 22, the Book of Lamentations, and John, chapters 14–17), pray the Rosary, or just sit quietly and peacefully in his presence. ✞

Good Friday
The second day of the Easter Triduum on which we have the Celebration of the Lord's Passion.

Article

48 Good Friday

Good Friday arrives as a solemn day, for it is the day on which we especially remember Christ's death, his love for us shown forth in his ultimate sacrifice. When we arrive at Church, it is stark; the altar is bare, the decorations have been removed, the statues are covered, and there is no holy water in the

The Church Prays

Lord,
by the suffering of Christ your Son
you have saved us all from the
    death
we inherited from sinful Adam.
By the law of nature
we have borne the likeness of his
    manhood.
May the sanctifying power of grace
help us to put on the likeness of
    our Lord in heaven,
who lives and reigns for ever and
    ever. Amen.

(Roman Missal)

© Brooklyn Museum/Corbis

fonts. This is a reminder of how we should approach this holy day—free from distractions so we can meditate on the reality of human sin and cruelty and the enormity of God's love.

Good Friday is both a day of sadness and a day of hope. It is a day of sadness because our sin made it necessary for Jesus to suffer and die. But it is a day of hope because through his death he has redeemed the world!

Liturgical Highlights

The Good Friday liturgy is called the Celebration of the Lord's Passion. The liturgy begins in silence, picking up where the Holy Thursday liturgy ended. It is usually held in the afternoon so that the time is close to the time of Christ's death, around 3:00 p.m.

The Liturgy of the Word

The readings in the liturgy focus on Christ's Passion. The Old Testament reading is a suffering servant song from Isaiah. The second reading is a reflection on the meaning of

Christ's suffering and death from the Letter to the Hebrews.
The Gospel account of Christ's arrest, mock trial, scourging,
and Crucifixion is from the Gospel of John. It is a long reading, and many parishes have speaking parts for the congregation. As the readings are proclaimed, really listen to them
and let them soak in and touch not just your mind but also
your heart.

venerate
To show respect and
devotion to someone
or something.

The Intercessions

The general intercessions are longer and more formal and
are usually sung on Good Friday. We pray for the Church,
the Pope, the clergy and laity, those preparing for Baptism,
the unity of Christians, the Jewish people, those who do not
believe in Christ or God, leaders in the world, and those in
special need. Listen carefully to these intercessions so you
can sincerely join in praying for these important needs.

The Veneration of the Cross

After the general intercessions, the priest brings up a cross
in solemn procession. Three times he lifts it up and sings,
"Behold the wood of the Cross, on which hung the salvation
of the world," and everyone responds "Come, let us adore."
Then the congregation is invited to come forward and
venerate the cross in some way. This is a way of showing our
deep appreciation for Christ's sacrifice. Some people kneel
or bow to the cross; some kiss or touch it. There may be a

As you par-
ticipate in the
veneration of
the cross on
Good Friday,
thank Christ for
his sacrificial
love. How will
you follow his
example of
loving sacrifice
for others?

© Bill Wittman/www.wpwittman.com

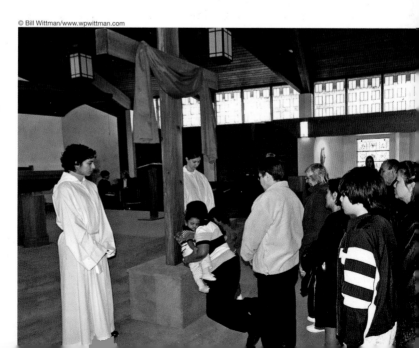

local custom to follow, but there is no right or wrong way to express your reverence. Whatever way you choose, let it come from your heart as an expression of your love for and devotion to Christ.

Communion

There is not a full Liturgy of the Eucharist on Good Friday. In a simple ritual, we receive the Body of Christ that was consecrated on Holy Thursday. After this the liturgy ends in silence, waiting to be concluded at the Easter Vigil the next night. As you receive the Body of Christ, be especially aware of his sacrifice, which enables us to live as the redeemed children of God.

Entering Into Sacred Time

Following are suggestions for ways you can more fully enter into the celebration of the Paschal Mystery, continuing into Good Friday:

Pray It!

Prayers for Good Friday

Lord, Send Your Abundant Blessing

Lord, send your abundant blessing upon your people
who devoutly recall the death of your Son
in the sure hope of the Resurrection.
Grant us pardon; bring us comfort.
May our faith grow stronger
and our eternal salvation be assured.

We Worship You, Lord

We worship you, Lord,
we venerate your cross
we praise your Resurrection.
Through the cross you brought joy to the world.

Holy Is God!

Holy is God!
Holy and strong!
Holy immortal One,
have mercy on us!

(Catholic Household Blessings and Prayers)

- Make a plan to attend the Celebration of the Lord's Passion. Find out the time it begins and mark it on your calendar. Encourage your family and friends to go too.

- This is an especially important day to fast as a way of keeping your focus on Christ's sacrifice and in anticipation of the celebration of the Resurrection. The Church asks us to eat only one full meal this day (for those between the ages 14 and 59) and to abstain from eating meat (required of all those over age 14). Decide what is possible for you based on your health needs, but make it a sacrifice.

- In some parishes and cities, the **Stations of the Cross** is also celebrated on Good Friday. In some places this is done very publicly, held outdoors and stopping at places that symbolize where Christ still suffers in the lives of people today. Find out if there is a Stations of the Cross in your area and attend if you can. It is a very moving remembrance of Christ's Passion.

- In the general intercessions, we pray for the spiritual and physical needs of the whole world. Take some time to pray for the needs of people who are close to you and who are in your community: people who are sick or hurting or without work or who don't know Christ.

- Spend some time reflecting on the mystery of Christ's Passion using the Bible. You may wish to read and reflect on the readings for the liturgy: Isaiah 52:13—53:12; Psalm 31; Hebrews 4:14–16, 5:7–9; John 18:1—19:42. Or look for other readings that talk about the meaning of Christ's suffering and death, such as Philippians 2:1–11 or Romans, chapter 5. ✝

Stations of the Cross
Images based on fourteen events in the Passion of Christ found on display in most Catholic churches. Also the devotional practice of private or communal prayer using these fourteen stations.

Article 49 The Easter Vigil

When we celebrate the Triduum as a kind of retreat, Holy Saturday arrives with a hint of excitement. The sadness of the Passion has passed, and we anticipate the celebration of Christ's victory over sin and death in the Easter Vigil liturgy. Yet it is still a day for reflection, meditation, and even rest. When the Easter Vigil arrives that night, you will want to be fully alert to truly appreciate and enter into the many won-

The Church Prays

Dear brothers and sisters,
on this most sacred night,
in which our Lord Jesus Christ
passed over from death to life,
the Church calls upon her sons and
     daughters,
scattered throughout the world,
to come together to watch and pray.
If we keep the memorial
of the Lord's paschal solemnity in
     this way,
listening to his word and celebrating
     his mysteries,
then we shall have the sure hope
of sharing his triumph over death
and living with him in God.

(Beginning of the Easter Vigil)

derful signs and symbols that comprise this beautiful liturgy that begins our Easter celebration.

Exult, let them exult, the hosts of heaven,
exult, let Angel ministers of God exult,
let the trumpet of salvation
sound aloud our mighty King's triumph!

(Easter Proclamation)

Easter Vigil Highlights

Easter is such an important feast day in the Christian calendar that it is not celebrated with just one liturgy. Easter begins with the celebration of the **Easter Vigil,** which many consider the highlight of the liturgical year. *Vigil* literally means "to be awake, to be watchful," and it is the name we give to liturgies held the night before an important feast. The Easter Vigil begins sometime after dark on Holy Saturday and must be finished before daybreak on Easter Sunday. The

celebration of Easter continues with the Mass of Easter Sunday. If you have never attended the Easter Vigil, make plans to do so; it is a beautiful, joyful, and powerful celebration of the Resurrection, the culmination of God's saving plan. Here are some of the highlights of this special liturgy.

The Service of Light

The Easter Vigil begins in darkness, outside the church if at all possible. A fire is lit and the priest welcomes us. The fire is blessed and the large **Easter candle** is lit. Then we process into the church, lighting our individual candles from the Easter candle. When all the candles are lit, the church is aglow with a beautiful and radiant light. The light of Christ has broken through the darkness of sin and death, illuminating our lives with holy light! As the Easter proclamation (also called the Exultet) is sung, look around at the people surrounding you and praise God in your heart for his saving love.

The Liturgy of the Word

The Liturgy of the Word in the Easter Vigil is very special. There are three to seven readings from the Old Testament and two from the New Testament. The readings provide an overview of salvation history, beginning with the creation of the world and culminating in the discovery of the empty tomb on Easter morning. You have studied God's saving

Easter Vigil
The liturgy celebrated on Holy Saturday night. It celebrates the coming of the light of Christ into the world and is also the time when adults and older children joining the Church receive the Sacraments of Christian Initiation.

Easter candle
A large candle symbolizing the light of Christ that is first lit at the Easter Vigil and then is lit for all the liturgies during the Easter Season. It is also called the Paschal candle.

During the Easter Vigil, catechumens complete their initiation in receiving the Sacraments of Baptism, Confirmation, and Holy Eucharist. How can their new commitment to Christ and his Church renew and strengthen your own commitment?

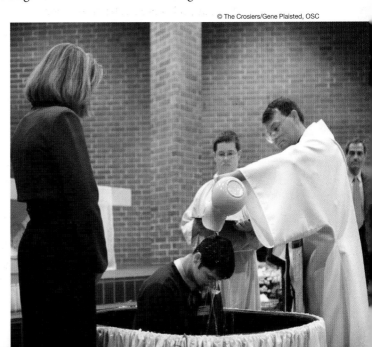

litany of the saints
A prayer in the form of a chant or a responsive petition in which the great saints of the Church are asked to pray for us.

plan in this book; now listen with new appreciation as it is proclaimed.

The Celebration of Baptism and Confirmation

After the homily the people who are ready to be brought into the Body of Christ receive the first two Sacraments of Christian Initiation: Baptism and Confirmation. We have seen these people throughout the year in the special rituals that prepared them for this night. We begin by singing the **litany of the saints,** a chant that reminds us that we are part of the Communion of Saints and that asks the saints in Heaven to join their prayers with ours. Then the priest or bishop baptizes those who are joining the Church. Next we hear the profession of faith from the people who have already been baptized and are now being received into full communion with the Catholic Church. They and the newly baptized are then confirmed. As you witness this part of the liturgy, let yourself share in the joy of these new Catholics. Let their commitment to our faith renew and strengthen your own commitment.

Liturgy of the Eucharist

We now move into the celebration of the Eucharist. Our Easter fast is over, and we break it by consuming the Body and Blood of Christ, our spiritual food and drink. This will be the first Eucharist for those who have just been baptized or were just received into the Church. We receive Jesus into our bodies, into our hearts, to nourish us and strengthen us. It is a time to be happy and rejoice; death has been conquered and eternal life awaits us. Our journey to holiness continues,

Catholic Wisdom

Love Is Stronger Than Death

Famous spiritual writer Henri Nouwen offers us this thoughtful reflection on the meaning of Jesus' Resurrection:

The Resurrection of Jesus was a hidden event (from those without faith). Jesus didn't rise from the grave to baffle his opponents, to make a victory statement, or to prove to those who crucified him that he was right after all. Jesus rose as a sign to those who had loved him and followed him that God's divine love is stronger than death.

but in this moment we are given a taste of the communion with God and the saints that awaits us in Heaven.

Entering into Sacred Time

Following are suggestions for ways you can more fully enter into the celebration of the Paschal Mystery, culminating in the Easter Vigil and Easter Sunday:

- Most parishes have a reception after the Easter Vigil to continue the celebration and meet the newly baptized and those received into the Church. Stay for the reception and introduce yourself to these new members of your community.
- Celebrate Easter with your family and friends. If you hunt Easter eggs, remember that eggs, chicks, and bunnies are associated with Easter because they are a sign of spring and of new life. Candy can be a sign of the sweetness of God's gift of salvation. A big Easter dinner is a sign that you are breaking the fasting of Lent and the Triduum.
- Your celebration does not have to end with the Easter Vigil. Consider attending the Mass again on Easter Sunday, when a different set of readings will be proclaimed. Or attend evening prayer on Easter Sunday if your parish celebrates that liturgy.
- It is always a good idea to take a few minutes on Easter Sunday for some praise and thanksgiving prayer. You might want to listen to some of your favorite Christian songs or hymns. Some Scripture passages you might want to meditate on are the Resurrection accounts in the Gospel of John (see chapters 20–21), Paul's reflection on resurrection (see 1 Corinthians 15:1–34), and the reflection in Hebrews on following Jesus (see chapter 12). ✝

Part Review

1. When does the Church's liturgical year begin? Identify some of the major feasts and seasons celebrated during the year.

2. What is the difference between *the liturgy* and *a liturgy?*

3. Why does the priest wash people's feet on Holy Thursday at the Mass of the Lord's Supper?

4. Describe the closing ritual at the end of the Mass of the Lord's Supper.

5. Why is Good Friday both a day of sadness and a day of hope?

6. What does *venerate* mean? Why do we venerate the cross at the Celebration of the Lord's Passion? How do people do it?

7. How does the Liturgy of the Word celebrated at the Easter Vigil differ from the Liturgy of the Word celebrated at Sunday Mass throughout the year?

8. What is the relationship between the Easter Vigil and the initiation of new members into the Church?

Glossary

A

adoration: The prayerful acknowledgement that God is God and Creator of all that is. *(page 187)*

analogy of faith: The coherence of individual doctrines with the whole of Revelation. In other words, as each doctrine is connected with Revelation, each doctrine is also connected with all other doctrines. *(page 64)*

angel: Based on a word meaning "messenger," a personal and immortal creature with intelligence and free will who constantly glorifies God and serves as a messenger of God to humans to carry out God's saving plan. *(page 16)*

Annunciation: The event in which the Archangel Gabriel came to Mary to announce that she had found favor with God and would become the mother of the Messiah. *(page 58)*

anthropomorphic: Attributing human characteristics to something that is not human. *(page 22)*

Apostles: The general term *apostle* means "one who is sent" and can be used in reference to any missionary of the Church during the New Testament period. In reference to the twelve companions chosen by Jesus, also known as "the Twelve," the term refers to those special witnesses of Jesus on whose ministry the early Church was built and whose successors are the bishops. *(page 98)*

archaeology: The scientific study of the material remains of past human life. *(page 11)*

Ark of the Covenant: A sacred chest that housed the tablets of the Ten Commandments. It was placed within the sanctuary where God would come and dwell. *(page 46)*

Ascension: The "going up" into Heaven of the Risen Christ forty days after his Resurrection. *(page 126)*

B

Baptism: The first of the Seven Sacraments, by which one becomes a member of the Church and a new creature in Christ; the first of the three Sacraments of Christian Initiation, the others being Confirmation and the Eucharist. *(page 19)*

beatific vision: Directly encountering and seeing God in the glory of Heaven. *(page 137)*

blasphemy: Speech or actions that show disrespect or irreverence for God; also, claiming to have the powers of God or to be God. *(page 103)*

blessing: A prayer asking God to care for a particular person, place, or activity. A simple blessing is usually made with the Sign of the Cross. *(page 187)*

225

C

cardinal virtues: Based on the Latin word for "pivot," four virtues that are viewed as pivotal or essential for full Christian living: prudence, justice, fortitude, and temperance. *(page 178)*

catechesis, catechists: Catechesis is the process by which Christians of all ages are taught the essentials of Christian doctrine and are formed as disciples of Christ. Catechists instruct others in Christian doctrine and for entry into the Church. *(page 163)*

chaplains: Specially prepared priests to whom the spiritual care of a special group of people, such as hospital patients, military personnel, or migrants, is entrusted. *(page 92)*

charity: The theological virtue by which we love God above all things and, out of that love of God, love our neighbors as ourselves. *(page 192)*

chastity: The virtue by which people are able to successfully and healthfully integrate their sexuality into their total person; recognized as one of the fruits of the Holy Spirit. Also one of the vows of religious life. *(page 87)*

chief priests: These were Jewish priests of high rank in the Temple. They had administrative authority and presided over important Temple functions and were probably leaders in the Sanhedrin. *(page 98)*

Chrism Mass: A special Mass usually celebrated during Holy Week in each diocese. During the Mass the bishop blesses the sacred oils and consecrates the Sacred Chrism used throughout the year, and diocesan priests renew their promises to their bishop. *(page 212)*

Christ: See *Jesus Christ.*

Christological: Having to do with the branch of theology called Christology. Christology is the study of the person and life of Jesus Christ, his ministry, and his mission. *(page 62)*

circumcision: The act, required by Jewish law, of removing the foreskin of the penis. Since the time of Abraham, it has been a sign of God's Covenant relationship with the Jewish people. *(page 44)*

clement: Merciful. *(page 59)*

concupiscence: The tendency of all human beings toward sin, as a result of Original Sin. *(page 30)*

confederation: An alliance of tribes or nations with no central authority. *(page 49)*

conscience: The "interior voice" of a person, a God-given sense of the law of God. Moral conscience leads people to understand themselves as responsible for their actions, and prompts them to do good and avoid evil. To make good judgments, one needs to have a well-formed conscience. *(page 85)*

consecrate: To declare or set apart as sacred or to solemnly dedicate to God's service; to make holy. *(page 151)*

contemplation: A form of wordless prayer in which one is fully focused on the presence of God; sometimes defined as "resting in God." *(page 195)*

corruptible: Something that can be spoiled or contaminated or made rotten, especially to be made morally perverted. *(page 119)*

D

doxology: The Christian prayers of praise that are usually directed to the Trinity. *(page 192)*

E

Easter candle: A large candle symbolizing the light of Christ that is first lit at the Easter Vigil and then is lit for all the liturgies during the Easter Season. It is also called the Paschal candle. *(page 221)*

Easter Vigil: The liturgy celebrated on Holy Saturday night. It celebrates the coming of the light of Christ into the world and is also the time when adults and older children joining the Church receive the Sacraments of Christian Initiation. *(page 220)*

etiology: A story that explains something's cause or origin. *(page 28)*

Eucharist, the: Also called the Mass or Lord's Supper, and based on a word for "thanksgiving," it is the central Christian liturgical celebration, established by Jesus at the Last Supper. In the Eucharist the sacrificial death and Resurrection of Jesus are both remembered and renewed. The term sometimes refers specifically to the consecrated bread and wine that have become the Body and Blood of Christ. *(page 77)*

exegesis: The study and proper interpretation of the Scriptures. *(page 123)*

Exile, the: The period of the Israelite captivity in Babylon after the destruction of Jerusalem in 587 BC. *(page 41)*

exorcism: The act of freeing someone from demonic possession. Exorcisms are also part of the Church's worship and prayer life, calling on the name of Christ to protect us from the power of Satan. *(page 91)*

expiation: The act of atoning for sin or wrongdoing. *(page 65)*

F

faith: In general, the belief in the existence of God. For Christians, the gift of God by which one freely accepts God's full Revelation in Jesus Christ. It is a matter of both the head (acceptance of God's revealed truth) and the heart (love of God and neighbor as a response to God's first loving us); also, one of the three theological virtues. *(page 12)*

Fall, the: Also called the Fall from grace, the biblical Revelation about the origins of sin and evil in the world, expressed figuratively in the account of Adam and Eve in Genesis. *(page 27)*

figurative language: A literary form that uses symbolic images, stories, and names to point to a deeper truth. *(page 12)*

foreshadow: To represent or prefigure a person before his or her life or an event before it occurs. *(page 62)*

fortitude: Also called strength or courage, the virtue that enables one to maintain sound moral judgment and behavior in the face of difficulties and challenges; one of the four cardinal virtues. *(page 178)*

G

gnosticism: A group of heretical religious movements that claimed salvation comes from secret knowledge available only to the elite initiated in that religion. *(page 116)*

Good Friday: The second day of the Easter Triduum on which we have the Celebration of the Lord's Passion. *(page 215)*

Gospel: Translated from a Greek word meaning "good news," referring to the four books attributed to Matthew, Mark, Luke, and John, "the principal source for the life and teaching of the Incarnate Word" (*CCC*, 125) Jesus Christ. *(page 113)*

grace: The free and undeserved gift of God's loving and active presence in our lives, empowering us to respond to his call and to live as his adopted sons and daughters. Grace restores our loving communion with the Holy Trinity, lost through sin. *(page 153)*

H

Heaven: A state of eternal life and union with God in which one experiences full happiness and the satisfaction of the deepest human longings. *(page 144)*

Hell: The eternal punishment of separation from God, reserved for those who die in mortal sin and are unrepentant, thus freely and consciously rejecting God at the end of their lives. *(page 146)*

hermit: A person who lives a solitary life in order to commit himself or herself more fully to prayer and in some cases to be completely free for service to others. *(page 158)*

holiness: The state of being holy. This means to be set apart for God's service, to live a morally good life, to be a person of prayer, and to reveal God's love to the world through acts of loving service. *(page 151)*

Holy Spirit: The Third Person of the Blessed Trinity, understood as the perfect love between God the Father, and the Son, Jesus Christ, who inspires, guides, and sanctifies the life of believers. *(page 11)*

Holy Thursday: The beginning of the Easter Triduum, starting with the evening celebration of the Mass of the Lord's Supper. *(page 212)*

hope: The theological virtue by which we trust in the promise of God and expect from God both eternal life and the grace we need to attain it; the conviction that God's grace is at work in the world and that the Kingdom of God established by and through Jesus Christ is becoming realized through the workings of the Holy Spirit among us. *(page 53)*

I

Immaculate Conception: The dogma that Mary was conceived without Original Sin and remained free from personal sin throughout her entire life. *(page 59)*

Incarnation: From the Latin, meaning "to become flesh," referring to the biblical Revelation that Jesus is both true God and true man. *(page 64)*

institute: To introduce, establish, or inaugurate. *(page 77)*

intercession: A prayer on behalf of another person or group. *(page 189)*

interiority: The practice of developing a life of self-reflection and self-examination to attend to your spiritual life and your call to holiness. *(page 154)*

J

Jesus Christ: The Son of God, the Second Person of the Trinity, who assumed human nature. *Jesus* in Hebrew means "God saves" and was the name given the historical Jesus at the Annunciation. *Christ*, the Greek translation of the word "Messiah," means "the anointed one," and is a title the Church gave Jesus after his full identity was revealed. *(page 15)*

K

Kingdom of God: The culmination or goal of God's plan of salvation, the Kingdom of God is announced by the Gospel and present in Jesus Christ. The Kingdom is the reign or rule of God over the hearts of people and, as a consequence of that, the development of a new social order based on unconditional love. The fullness of God's Kingdom will not be realized until the end of time. Also called the Reign of God or the Kingdom of Heaven. *(page 74)*

L

laity: All members of the Church with the exception of those who are ordained as bishops, priests, or deacons. The laity share in Christ's role as priest, prophet, and king, witnessing to God's love and power in the world. *(page 155)*

legalistic: To focus strictly on what the law requires without considering the truth the law is intended to promote. Jesus taught that all law must be an expression of love for God and love for our neighbor. *(page 85)*

leprosy: An infectious disease resulting in numbness, paralysis, and physical deformities; also called Hansen's disease. Effective treatment was not developed until the late 1930s. *(page 176)*

litany of the saints: A prayer in the form of a chant or a responsive petition in which the great saints of the Church are asked to pray for us. *(page 222)*

literal sense: A form of biblical interpretation that considers the explicit meaning of the text. It lays the foundation for all other senses of the Scriptures. *(page 37)*

literary forms (genres): Different kinds of writing determined by their literary technique, content, tone, and purpose (how the author wants the reader to be affected). *(page 13)*

liturgical year: The annual cycle of religious feasts and seasons that forms the context for the Church's worship. During the liturgical year, we remember and celebrate God the Father's saving plan as it is revealed through the life of his Son, Jesus Christ. *(page 207)*

liturgy: The Church's official, public, communal prayer. It is God's work, in which the People of God participate. The Church's most important liturgy is the Eucharist, or the Mass. *(page 207)*

Liturgy of the Hours: Also known as the Divine Office, the official public, daily prayer of the Catholic Church. The Divine Office provides standard prayers, Scripture readings, and reflections at regular hours throughout the day. *(page 207)*

Lord: The Old Testament name for God that in speaking or reading aloud was automatically substituted for the name *Yahweh*, which was considered too sacred to be spoken; in the New Testament, used for both God the Father and Jesus Christ, to reflect awareness of Jesus' divine identity as the Son of God. *(page 70)*

M

meditation: A form of prayer involving a variety of methods and techniques, in which one engages the mind, imagination, and emotions to focus on a particular truth, biblical theme, or other spiritual matter. *(page 194)*

monarchy: A government or a state headed by a single person, like a king or queen. As a biblical term, it refers to the period of time when the Israelites existed as an independent nation. *(page 50)*

mortal sin: An action so contrary to the will of God that it results in complete separation from God and his grace. As a consequence of that separation, the person is condemned to eternal death. For a sin to be a mortal sin, three conditions must be met: the act must involve grave matter, the person must have full knowledge of the evil of the act, and the person must give his or her full consent in committing the act. *(page 136)*

mysticism: An intense experience of the presence and power of God, resulting in a deeper sense of union with God; those who regularly experience such union are called mystics. *(page 196)*

O

Oil of the Catechumens: Blessed olive oil used to anoint those preparing for Baptism. *(page 212)*

Oil of the Sick: Blessed olive oil used in the Sacrament of Anointing of the Sick to anoint the forehead and hands of people who are seriously ill or near death. *(page 212)*

original holiness: The original state of human beings in their relationship with God, sharing in the divine life in full communion with him. *(page 22)*

original justice: The state of complete harmony of our first parents with themselves, with each other, and with all of creation. *(page 22)*

Original Sin: From the Latin *origo*, meaning "beginning" or "birth." The term has two meanings: (1) the sin of the first human beings, who disobeyed God's command by choosing to follow their own will and so lost their original holiness and became subject to death, (2) the fallen state of human nature that affects every person born into the world. *(page 29)*

P

paradox: A statement that seems contradictory or opposed to common sense and yet is true. *(page 129)*

Parousia: The second coming of Christ at the end of time, fully realizing God's plan and the glorification of humanity. *(page 33)*

Paschal Lamb: In the Old Testament, the sacrificial lamb shared at the seder meal of the Passover on the night the Israelites escaped from Egypt; in the New Testament, the Paschal Lamb is Jesus, the Suffering Servant of God who dies on a cross to take away "the sin of the world" (John 1:29). *(page 77)*

Paschal Mystery: The work of salvation accomplished by Jesus Christ mainly through his life, Passion, death, Resurrection, and Ascension. *(page 41)*

Passion: The sufferings of Jesus during his final days in this life: his agony in the garden at Gethsemane, his trial, and his Crucifixion. *(page 97)*

Passover: The night the Lord passed over the houses of the Israelites marked by the blood of the lamb, and spared the firstborn sons from death. It also is the feast that celebrates the deliverance of the Chosen People from bondage in Egypt and the Exodus from Egypt to the Promised Land. *(page 77)*

patriarch: The father or leader of a tribe, clan, or tradition. Abraham, Isaac, and Jacob were the patriarchs of the Israelite people. *(page 44)*

petition: A prayer form in which one asks God for help and forgiveness. *(page 188)*

polytheism: The belief in many gods. *(page 42)*

poverty of heart: The recognition of our deep need for God and the commitment to put God above everything else in life, particularly above the accumulation of material wealth. *(page 80)*

praise: A prayer of acknowledgment that God is God, giving God glory not for what he does, but simply because he is. *(page 191)*

prayer: Lifting up of one's mind and heart to God in praise, petition, thanksgiving, and intercession; communication with God in a relationship of love. *(page 185)*

primeval history: The time before the invention of writing and recording of historical data. *(page 11)*

procurator: A word used to describe Roman governors. These men had administrative and legal authority over a province or region of the Roman Empire. *(page 103)*

Purgatory: A state of final purification or cleansing, which one may need to enter following death and before entering Heaven. *(page 147)*

R

redeem, Redeemer, redemption: From the Latin *redemptio,* meaning "a buying back;" to redeem something is to pay the price for its freedom. In the Old Testament, it refers to Yahweh's deliverance of Israel and, in the New Testament, to Christ's deliverance of all Christians from the forces of sin. Christ our Redeemer paid the price to free us from the slavery of sin and bring about our redemption. *(page 78)*

Resurrection: The passage of Jesus from death to new life "on the third day" after his Crucifixion; the heart of the Paschal Mystery and the basis of our hope in the resurrection from the dead. *(page 113)*

resurrection of the dead: The Christian dogma that all those deemed righteous by God will be raised and will live forever with God in Heaven; the conviction that not only our souls but also our transformed bodies will live on after death. *(page 118)*

righteous: To be sinless and without guilt before God. Can also be used as a noun. *(page 125)*

S

Sacrament: An efficacious and visible sign of God's invisible grace, instituted by Christ. The Seven Sacraments are Baptism, the Eucharist, Confirmation, Penance and Reconciliation, Anointing of the Sick, Matrimony, and Holy Orders. *(page 208)*

Sacred Chrism: Perfumed olive oil that has been consecrated. It is used for anointing in the Sacraments of Baptism, Confirmation, and Holy Orders. *(page 212)*

saint: Someone who has been transformed by the grace of Christ and who resides in full union with God in Heaven. *(page 44)*

sanctifying grace: The grace that heals our human nature wounded by sin and restores us to friendship with God by giving us a share in the divine life of the Trinity. It is a supernatural gift of God, infused into our souls by the Holy Spirit, that continues the work of making us holy. *(page 139)*

Sanhedrin: An assembly of Jewish religious leaders—chief priests, rabbis, scribes, and elders—who functioned as the supreme council and tribunal during the time of Christ. *(page 99)*

Satan: The fallen angel or spirit of evil who is the enemy of God and a continuing instigator of temptation and sin in the world. *(page 31)*

Scripture(s): Generally, the term for any sacred writing. For Christians, the Old and New Testaments that make up the Bible and are recognized as the Word of God. *(page 11)*

Son of God: Title frequently applied to Jesus Christ, which recognizes him as the Second Person of the Blessed Trinity. *(page 19)*

soul: Our spiritual principle, it is immortal, and it is what makes us most like God. Our soul is created by God. It is the seat of human consciousness and freedom. *(page 17)*

spirituality: In general, the values, actions, attitudes, and behaviors that characterize a person's relationship with God and others. In particular, it refers to different schools of Christian prayer and action. *(page 201)*

spiritual sense: A form of biblical interpretation that goes beyond the literal sense to consider what the realities and events of the Scriptures signify and mean for salvation. *(page 37)*

Stations of the Cross: Images based on fourteen events in the Passion of Christ found on display in most Catholic churches. Also the devotional practice of private or communal prayer using these fourteen stations. *(page 219)*

T

thanksgiving: A prayer of gratitude for the gift of life and the gifts of life. Thanksgiving characterizes the prayer of the Church which, in celebrating the Eucharist, offers perfect thanks to the Father through, with, and in Christ, in the unity of the Holy Spirit. *(page 190)*

theological virtues: The name for the God-given virtues of faith, hope, and love. These virtues enable us to know God as God and lead us to union with him in mind and heart. *(page 139)*

theophany: God's breaking into the human dimension so an individual's and community's understanding of God is deepened or changed. *(page 45)*

Theotokos: A Greek title for Mary meaning "God bearer." *(page 58)*

Torah: A Hebrew word meaning "law," referring to the first five books of the Old Testament. *(page 46)*

Tradition: This word (from the Latin, meaning "to hand on") refers to the process of passing on the Gospel message. Tradition, which began with the oral communication of the Gospel by the Apostles, was written down in the Scriptures, is handed down and lived out in the life of the Church, and is interpreted by the Magisterium under the guidance of the Holy Spirit. *(page 15)*

Triduum: The three-day period of the liturgical year that begins with the Mass of the Lord's Supper on Holy Thursday and ends with evening prayer on Easter Sunday. *(page 209)*

Trinity: From the Latin *trinus*, meaning "threefold," referring to the central mystery of the Christian faith that God exists as a communion of three distinct and interrelated divine Persons: Father, Son, and Holy Spirit. The doctrine of the Trinity is a mystery that is inaccessible to human reason alone and is known through Divine Revelation only. *(page 15)*

V

venerate: To show respect and devotion to someone or something. *(page 217)*

venial sin: A less serious offense against the will of God that diminishes one's personal character and weakens but does not rupture one's relationship with God. *(page 136)*

virtue: A habitual and firm disposition to do good. *(page 178)*

vocal prayer: A prayer that is spoken aloud or silently, such as the Lord's Prayer. *(page 194)*

Index

Page numbers in italics refer to illustrations.

Acknowledgments

The scriptural quotations in this book are from the New American Bible with Revised New Testament and Revised Psalms. Copyright © 1991, 1986, and 1970 by the Confraternity of Christian Doctrine, Washington, D.C. Used by the permission of the copyright owner. All rights reserved. No part of the New American Bible may be reproduced in any form without permission in writing from the copyright owner.

The excerpts marked *Catechism of the Catholic Church* or *CCC* are from the English translation of the *Catechism of the Catholic Church* for use in the United States of America, second edition. Copyright © 1994 by the United States Catholic Conference, Inc.—Libreria Editrice Vaticana. English translation of the *Catechism of the Catholic Church: Modifications from the Editio Typica* copyright © 1997 by the United States Catholic Conference, Inc.—Libreria Editrice Vaticana.

Some of the definitions in this book are taken or adapted from *The Catholic Faith Handbook for Youth*, Second Edition, by Brian Singer-Towns (Winona, MN: Saint Mary's Press, 2008). Copyright © 2008 by Saint Mary's Press. All rights reserved.

The excerpt on page 12 is from "Address of His Holiness Benedict XVI to the Members of the Pontifical Academy of Sciences," at *www.vatican. va/holy_father/benedict_xvi/speeches/2006/november/documents/hf_ben-xvi_spe_20061106_academy-sciences_en.html*. Copyright © 2006—Libreria Editrice Vaticana.

The prayers on pages 21, 37, 211, 217, and 220 are from the English translation of *The Roman Missal* © 2010, International Commission on English in the Liturgy (ICEL). English translation prepared by the ICEL. All rights reserved. Used with permission of the ICEL.

The prayer on page 216 is from The Roman Missal © 1973, ICEL. English translation prepared by the ICEL (New York: Catholic Book Publishing Company, 1985), page 140. Illustrations and arrangement copyright © 1985–1974 by the Catholic Book Publishing Company, New York. Used with permission of the ICEL.

The excerpt on page 30 is from *Pastoral Constitution on the Church in the Modern World* (*Gaudium et Spes*, 1965), number 16, at *www.vatican.va/ archive/hist_councils/ii_vatican_council/documents/vat-ii_cons_19651207_ gaudium-et-spes_en.html*. Copyright © Libreria Editrice Vaticana.

The excerpt on page 40 is from Saint Leo the Great, "Sermon 73," number IV, found at *www.newadvent.org/fathers/360373.htm*.

The excerpt on page 53 is from "Encyclical Letter *Spe Salvi* of the Supreme Pontiff Benedict XVI to the Bishops, Priests and Deacons, Men and Women Religious, and all the Lay Faithful on Christian Hope," number 1, at *www.vatican.va/holy_father/benedict_xvi/encyclicals/documents/ hf_ben-xvi_enc_20071130_spe-salvi_en.html*. Copyright © 2007—Libreria Editrice Vaticana.

The excerpts on pages 67 and 84 are quoted from *The Faith of the Early Fathers*, volume one, selected and translated by W. A. Jurgens (Collegeville, MN: The Liturgical Press), pages 322 and 176. Copyright © 1970 by the Order of St. Benedict, Collegeville, MN.

The quotation on page 74 is from "Apostolic Letter *Rosarium Virginis Mariae* of the Supreme Pontiff John Paul II to the Bishops, Clergy and Faithful on the Most Holy Rosary," number 21, at *www.vatican.va/holy_ father/john_paul_ii/apost_letters/documents/hf_jp-ii_apl_20021016_ rosarium-virginis-mariae_en.html*. Copyright © Libreria Editrice Vaticana.

The excerpts on pages 79 and 174 are quoted from *Mother Teresa: Her Essential Wisdom*, edited by Carol Kelly-Gangi (New York: Barnes and Noble, 2006). Compilation copyright © 2006 by Barnes and Noble Publishing, Inc.

The excerpt on page 90 from *Pastoral Care of the Sick: Rites of Anointing and Viaticum* © 1982, ICEL, number 125; and the excerpt on page 147 from *Order of Christian Funerals* © 1985, ICEL, number 72, are found in *The Rites of the Catholic Church*, volume one, prepared by the ICEL, a Joint Commission of Catholic Bishops' Conferences (Collegeville, MN: The Liturgical Press, 1990). Copyright © 1990 by the Order of St. Benedict, Collegeville, MN. Used with permission of the ICEL.

The excerpt on page 102 is from *Declaration on the Relation of the Church to Non-Christian Religions* (*Nostra Aetate*, 1965), number 4, at *www.vatican.va/archive/hist_councils/ii_vatican_council/documents/vat- ii_decl_19651028_nostra-aetate_en.html*. Copyright © Libreria Editrice Vaticana.

The excerpt on page 106 is from *Julian of Norwich: Showings*, long text, chapter 5, translated from the critical text by Edmund Colledge and James Walsh (New York: Paulist Press), page 183. Copyright © 1978 by the Missionary Society of Saint Paul the Apostle in the State of New York.

The excerpts on pages 108–109, 123–124, and 193 are from the English translation of Sermons of the Fathers from *The Liturgy of the Hours* © 1974 ICEL, as quoted in *Touching the Risen Christ: Wisdom from The Fathers*, Patricia Mitchell, general editor (Ijamsville, MD: The Word Among Us Press, 1999), pages 69–71, 86–87, and 36–37, respectively. Copyright © 1999 by The Word Among Us Press. Used with permission of the ICEL.

The excerpt on page 132 is from *Hold Fast to God: Wisdom from the Early Church*, Jeanne Kun, editor (Ijamsville, MD: The Word Among Us

Press, 2001), pages 111 and 112–113. Copyright © 2001 by The Word Among Us Press.

The excerpt on page 145 is from "The Epistle of Ignatius to the Romans," chapter 6, found at *www.newadvent.org/fathers/0107.htm.*

The excerpt on page 156 is from *Dogmatic Constitution on the Church* (*Lumen Gentium*, 1964), numbers 10 and 31, at *www. vatican.va/archive/hist_councils/ii_vatican_council/documents/ vat-ii_const_19641121_lumen-gentium_en.html.*

The excerpt on page 184 is from *Gratefulness, the Heart of Prayer: An Approach to Life in Fullness,* by Br. David Steindl-Rast (New York: Paulist Press, 1984), page 41. Copyright © 1984 by David Steindl-Rast.

The prayers on page 218, copyright © 1973 ICEL, are reprinted from *Catholic Household Blessings and Prayers,* by the Bishops' Committee on the Liturgy (Washington, DC: United States Conference of Catholic Bishops [USCCB], 1989), page 146. Copyright © 1989 by the USCCB. All rights reserved. Used with permission of the ICEL.

The excerpt on page 222 is from *Bread for the Journey: A Daybook of Wisdom and Faith,* by Henri J. M. Nouwen (New York: HarperCollins, 1997), page 344. Copyright © 1997 by Henri J. M. Nouwen.

To view copyright terms and conditions for Internet materials cited here, log on to the home pages for the referenced Web sites.

During this book's preparation, all citations, facts, figures, names, addresses, telephone numbers, Internet URLs, and other pieces of information cited within were verified for accuracy. The authors and Saint Mary's Press staff have made every attempt to reference current and valid sources, but we cannot guarantee the content of any source, and we are not responsible for any changes that may have occurred since our verification. If you find an error in, or have a question or concern about, any of the information or sources listed within, please contact Saint Mary's Press.

Endnotes Cited in Quotations from the *Catechism of the Catholic Church*, Second Edition

Unit 3
1. *Romans* 6:4; cf. 4:25.
Unit 4
1. Cf. *2 Timothy* 4.
2. Cf. John Paul II, *Redemptor hominis* 18–21.